UNITE History
Volume 1 (1880–1931)

The Transport and General Workers' Union (TGWU):
Representing a Mass Trade Union Movement

UNITE History
Volume 1
(1880–1931)

The Transport and
General Workers' Union (TGWU):
Representing a Mass
Trade Union Movement

Mary Davis and John Foster

LIVERPOOL UNIVERSITY PRESS

First published 2021 by
Liverpool University Press
4 Cambridge Street
Liverpool
L69 7ZU

British Library Cataloguing-in-Publication data
A British Library CIP record is available

ISBN 978 1 80085 971 5

Typeset by Carnegie Book Production, Lancaster
Printed and bound by CPI Group (UK) Ltd, Croydon CR0 4YY

Contents

Figures

Boxes

Abbreviations

AATVW	Amalgamated Association of Tramway and Vehicle Workers
AEU	Amalgamated Engineering Union
ASE	Amalgamated Society of Engineers
ASLEF	Associated Society of Locomotive Engineers and Firemen
ATGWU	Amalgamated Transport and General Workers' Union (TGWU in Ireland)
BSP	British Socialist Party
CPGB	Communist Party of Great Britain
CSEC	Central Strike Executive Committee
CWC	Clyde Workers' Committee
CWS	Cooperative Wholesale Society
DORA	Defence of the Realm Act
DWRGLU	Dock, Wharf, Riverside and General Labourers' Union
GEC	General Executive Council
GMWU	General and Municipal Workers Union
GNCTU	Grand National Consolidated Trade Union
GUBA	Glasgow University Business Archives
HoR	Hands off Russia
IFTU	International Federation of Trade Unions
ILP	Independent Labour Party
ITGWU	Irish Transport and General Workers Union
JIC	Joint Industrial Councils
LGOC	London General Omnibus Company
LPU	London and Provincial Union of Licensed Vehicle Worker
LRC	Labour Representation Committee
MFGB	Miners' Federation of Great Britain
MML	Marx Memorial Library
MRC	Modern Records Centre, University of Warwick
NMM	National Minority Movement
NSFU	National Sailors' and Firemen's Union
NTWF	National Transport Workers Federation

NUDL	National Union of Dock Labourers
NUR	National Union of Railwaymen
NUS	National Union of Seamen
NUW(C)M	National Unemployed Workers' (Committee) Movement
NUWM	National Unemployed Workers Movement
OMS	Organisation for the Maintenance of Supply
OTC	Officer Training Corps
RILU	Red International of Labour Unions
STC	Supply and Transport Committee
STUC	Scottish Trades Union Congress
TA	Territorial Army
TGWU	Transport and General Workers Union
TNA	The National Archive
TUC	Trades Union Congress
UVW	United Vehicle Workers
WRC	Workers Representation Committee
WSPU	Women's Social and Political Union
WU	Workers' Union
WW1	World War One

Foreword

Unite History Project
The Six Volume History

The six volumes explore the history of the Transport and General Workers' Union (T&G) from its beginnings through to the formation of Unite the union with Amicus in 2007. Whilst each volume can be read on its own, as a stand-alone book, the series shares a set of overarching common themes. These themes run through every text, raising questions – and learning points for discussion – as we explore the different experiences of each historical period, co-producing knowledge with trade union education officers and activists working alongside academics on the basis of their shared researches.

Each volume aims to co-research and co-produce political education resources, building on experiences of political education in the past, focusing on histories of collective action, within a national framework, in order to:

- focus upon histories of collective action within a national historical context, reflecting upon past experiences of class struggles including experiences of international solidarity and of solidarity with communities and public service users

- investigate struggles for democracy and equalities for women, Black, Asian and Minority Ethnic (BAME) communities and LGTB people, both within the trade union and Labour movement and within the wider social context

- reflect on relationships between trade unions, employers and the state, with a particular focus on relationships with the Labour Party

- draw lessons from past achievements and mistakes to apply these critically to contemporary challenges, recognising past shortcomings as well as celebrating past achievements.

These themes run though all six volumes, with case studies of different struggles, for illustration. The ways in which we have been working together need to be emphasised – and celebrated. This has been a truly remarkable process. Our Unite regional teams have developed unique ways of bringing materials together, drawing on archival research, members' own experiences and identifying activists who have been prepared to share their stories of struggle. We have each brought our own knowledge and our own understandings, with shared commitments to critical enquiry, recognising mistakes and shortcomings as well as celebrating the trade union and Labour movement's remarkable achievements. All in all, this process has provided an extraordinary case study in its own right, illustrating ways in which collective working, historical research and oral histories can enrich the study of our labour history using both published and unpublished materials, co-producing knowledge as the basis for collective learning for social transformation.

Len McCluskey
General Secretary of Unite the Union

I

Origins and Formation 1880–1924

1

Setting the Scene 1880–1920

Which explains the militancy of the period, how new general unions were formed, the impact of World War One and the Russian Revolution

Trade Unionism 1880s–1920

Trade unions grew at a faster rate than at any time in their history between 1888 and 1920. The estimated membership figure stood at roughly 750,000 at the beginning of the period, rising to six and a half million in 1918. Up to this time trade unions (from the 1830s) had been open only to skilled male workers. During this period 'new unionism', as it came to be called, saw semi- and un-skilled workers, including women, join the ranks of organised labour. The spectacular growth took place in three main periods: from 1880–91; from 1910–14 during 'the great unrest', a period of extensive strike action largely inspired by syndicalism; and during the war years 1914–18, which not only continued the militancy of the previous four years but witnessed the development of the shop stewards' movement.

Trade unionism spread to previously unorganised workers and its initial militancy rocked the complacency of the old leadership. The new mood was inspired by a revival in socialist activity beginning in the 1880s. The revival of the political left began during the harsh climate following the ending of Britain's boom during its mid-century 'workshop of the world' phase, when British manufactured goods dominated world trade. However, this period (the last quarter of the nineteenth century) was one of adjustment rather than breakdown, in which the old labour–capital consensus, although shaken, was ultimately renewed.

The material basis for the capitalist state's ability to adjust was due to the massive expansion of the British Empire in the last quarter of the nineteenth century. The Empire helped to maintain low prices, especially of food, at a time of economic adversity, thus preventing a drastic drop in real wages for those who had jobs. By providing protected markets it assisted in the maintenance of high profits in certain traditional export industries (the staples: coal, cotton and engineering) which had lost their competitive edge elsewhere due to foreign competition from more recently industrialised countries like Germany and the US. The transport industry – comprising road, rail, canal docks and shipping – expanded rapidly in the 'age of Empire'. Massive technological advances in the source of motive power – steam, gas, petrol and later electricity – impacted on all industries, especially transport, which saw an increase in employment. Taken together transport workers comprised over 12 per cent of the British labour force – the highest proportion of any industrial sector.

New Unionism 1888–91 and the Great Dock Strike

It is against this background that the growth and development of trade unions in this period must be understood. This provides the context for the eventual emergence of the Transport and General Workers' Union in 1922.

The success of the Women Match Workers' strike at the Bryant and May factory in 1888 inspired two important disputes in the following year – the gasworkers' strike and the dockers' strike of 1889. Dockers in the Port of London struck work in support of their claim for 6d an hour and an end to casualisation (they demanded at least four hours a day continuous work). The strike lasted five weeks. Many other port workers followed the dockers' lead, including seamen, lightermen, watermen, rope makers, fish porters and carmen. Outside the docks, strikes broke out daily in factories and workshops throughout the East End of London, involving an estimated 130,000 workers. The dock strike was particularly signifi-cant for three reasons. Firstly because it was successful, having inspired and been sustained by national and international solidarity. Secondly, because it led to the formation of the Dock, Wharf, Riverside and General Labourers' Union (DWRGLU), which, as we shall see, became one of the most important unions in the TGWU amalgamation process. Thirdly, its success marked the beginning of what is now termed 'new unionism'. One of the strike organisers alongside Ben Tillett was Tom Mann, who in his 'Memoirs' wrote: 'The stimulus that the dock strike gave to trade unionism was very great, and far-reaching; it led to a real revival'.[1]

This revival witnessed the expansion of trade unionism among previously unorganised workers who had been excluded from the craft unions' dominance of the labour movement from the 1850s onwards. The term 'new unionism' does not simply refer to the fact that many new

1   T. Mann, *Memoirs* (Macgibbon & Kee, 1967), p.70.

unions were formed, but that a new approach to trade unionism permeated both the older and the new organisations. Tom Mann and Ben Tillett criticised the old outlook in a penny pamphlet, published in 1891:

> many of the older unions are very reluctant to engage in a labour struggle, no matter how great the necessity, because they are hemmed in by sick and funeral claims, so that to a large extent they have lost their true characteristic of being fighting organisations.[2]

The outlook of old unionism was challenged by class conscious socialists, some of whom – like Tom Mann and John Burns – were already, as members of the Amalgamated Society of Engineers (ASE), experienced trade unionists. The strike activity which led to the breakthrough among the unskilled was often led or inspired by socialists. Mann and Burns, both of whom played a key role among the dockers, were members of the Social Democratic Federation as was Will Thorne, the gasworkers' leader. Prominent socialists outside the trade union movement, like Eleanor Marx, Keir Hardie and H.H. Champion were frequent speakers at mass meetings of trade unionists and also assisted in recruitment drives. Eleanor Marx was particularly involved in the birth and growth of the National Union of Gasworkers and General Labourers in 1889. She worked closely alongside its general secretary, Will Thorne, who acknowledged her as his mentor.

The organising principle of new unionism was that of mass recruitment. Whereas old unionism had relied on the skill and scarcity value of labour, new unionism was dependent on sheer force of numbers for its success. Thus women were welcomed as members from the start, hence accounting for the first recorded real increase in women's trade union membership, from roughly 50,000 in 1888 to about 432,000 in 1913. The central slogan of this forward movement was that of the demand for an eight-hour day – a demand of the international labour movement, popularised by the newly formed International Socialist Congress, more commonly known as the Second International (1889–1914). The huge May Day demonstration of 1890 in favour of the eight-hour day took even its organisers by surprise.

Employers' Counter Offensive

Owing to the determined resistance of employers, aided by state legislative action, many of the new unions collapsed. This was the period in which determined efforts were made to counter trade union growth by more effective and co-ordinated employers' strategies, witnessed by the formation of employers' associations within – and ultimately across – industries, and

---

2 Quoted in M. Davis, *Comrade or Brother?* (Pluto Press, 2009), p.116.

their widespread adoption of the tactics of the lockout and the use of 'scab' labour. The first of their targets was the new unions. By these means even the biggest of the new unions – the gasworkers' union and the dockers' union – were temporarily broken. The job of breaking the older unions was not so easy, but it was even more vital for the employers so to do. Trade union resistance in the staple industries (coal, cotton and engineering) was delaying employer determination to introduce new work methods and wage cutting associated with the drive for labour intensification – their preferred strategy, in the absence of capital investment, to ensure the maintenance of their profits in an increasingly competitive world market. Thus it was that attempts were made by the employers to reduce wages in the cotton and mining industries in 1893 and to defeat the engineers' struggle for the eight-hour day following the national lockout of 1897. The settlement which ended the cotton spinners' strike and the engineers' lockout resulted in a form of collective bargaining which incorporated the unions' leaderships in an industrial truce that implicitly acknowledged the main objective of the employers – the 'right to manage' at a time of great internal change in their industries. The 1893 Brooklands Agreement (cotton) was the prototype. It established a National Procedure Agreement whereby all disputes at a national or local level had to be referred to a central joint council of the industry (consisting of union and management sides) before strike action was 'permitted'. Other industries apart from engineering followed suit – the boot and shoe industry in 1895, the building industry in 1904 and shipbuilding in 1908. This new departure in industrial relations also helps to explain the period of industrial peace between 1888 and 1907. The practice of employer–worker co-operation continued to be influential in the twentieth century. Indeed in 1917, Ernest Bevin, then leader of the Bristol dockers, was vice-chair of the Bristol Association for Industrial Reconstruction, the aim of which was 'to foster & maintain a better spirit in industrial life [...] and [thus] removing the causes which tend to create distrust & suspicion between employers and employees'.[3]

On the face of it therefore, it seemed that by the twentieth century, trade unionism had achieved very little. The gains of the old leadership had been undone both by the courts and by the fluctuations of the economy, and the new unions had little to show for themselves with the exception of the new and continuing organisation of white-collar and professional workers. The only new union to be formed during the period of industrial peace was an unlikely but significant one in that it foreshadowed the ideas which inspired 'the great unrest'. This was the as yet tiny Workers' Union, formed in 1898 by Tom Mann as a general union along the lines of the old Grand National Consolidated Trade Union (GNCTU) of 1834. Trade

---

3 Modern Records Centre (MRC), University of Warwick. MSS.126/EB/X/36. Bevin Papers private correspondence, 1916–17.

union membership, which stood at just over two million in 1900, actually declined slightly between 1903 and 1906. However, the lull in trade union militancy was short-lived. The hostility of the employers to trade unionism was reinforced by two infamous legal decisions. The case of Lyons vs Wilkins in 1896 set a precedent for outlawing even peaceful picketing. The Taff Vale judgment of 1901 ruled that the employer (the Taff Vale Railway Company) could sue the union (in this case the Amalgamated Society of Railway Servants) for losses sustained during a strike. Thus a precedent was set for effectively preventing strike action altogether.

The Labour Party

In a practical sense, the Taff Vale decision of 1901 was more important in convincing the trade unions of the need for a parliamentary voice than countless socialist exhortations on the bankruptcy of liberalism, to which unions had been wedded since the second Reform Act of 1867. This Act enfranchised the better-paid skilled workers whose support for the Liberal Party was secured by of allowing such workers to stand for parliament as Liberal candidates. This practice was known as 'lib-labism'. By 1884 two-thirds of adult males had the vote and thus some unions and the Independent Labour Party (ILP), founded in 1893, argued that workers should have independent labour representation in parliament. Thus the Labour Representation Committee (LRC) was formed in 1900, in order 'to establish a distinct labour group in parliament who shall have their own whips and agree upon their own policy'.[4] This relatively limited objective was hard to achieve given the trade union leaderships' attachment to liberalism, and could only be accomplished by an appeal to pragmatism rather than idealism; Taff Vale was the catalyst. Unions now saw that it was essential to have a voice in parliament in order to reverse this judgment and to guarantee unions immunity during an industrial dispute. Within two years the affiliated membership of the LRC, now called the Labour Party, had doubled. By 1906 it had returned 29 MPs to Parliament. Keir Hardie of the ILP characterised the 'philosophy' of the new organisation not as socialism but as *labourism* which he defined as:

> Theory and practice which accepted the possibility of social change within the existing framework of society; which rejected the revolutionary violence and action implicit in Chartist ideas of physical force; and which increasingly recognised the working of political democracy of the parliamentary variety as the practical means of achieving its own aims and objectives.[5]

4 Quoted in Davis, *Comrade or Brother?*, p.132.
5 Ibid., p.133.

The 'Great Unrest' 1910–14 and Syndicalism

From 1910 until the outbreak of war, the number of working days lost in strikes rose to an annual total of more than ten million or more, while membership of trade unions rose from two-and-a-half million workers in 1910 to four million by 1914. This growth was a product of the extraordinary militancy of the pre-war years which exploded in a huge wave of strike action, dubbed 'the great unrest'. It owed little to leadership of the industrial and political wings of the labour movement; indeed its very hostility to such leadership, which was condemned as class collaborationist, inspired its alternative – syndicalism. The vacuum created by the absence of political leadership from the Labour Party, together with the ineffectiveness of old unionism meant that syndicalism, with its clarion call to direct action by the rank and file, found a ready response within the conditions of pre-war industrial militancy.

Tom Mann was a leading advocate of this new trend. Although a minority current in the labour movement, syndicalists offered a simple alternative to the continued employers' offensive – that of direct action in order to regain some form of workers' control over workplace pay and conditions utilising the strategy of the mass strike and rapid trade union recruitment. In 1910 Mann was invited by Tillett to speak to the Dockers' Union (DWRGLU) about industrial unionism among transport workers. Syndicalists regarded transport workers, with their multiplicity of unions, as prime candidates for 'one big union'. Indeed, the 1910 issue of *Industrial Syndicalist* (edited by Tom Mann) was entirely devoted to the transport industry. This resulted later in the year in the federation of 15 unions leading to the formation, clearly inspired by syndicalism, of the National Transport Workers' Federation (NTWF). The NTWF was later to be a key component of the TGWU. By 1912 the affiliated membership of the NTWF was 220,000. Ernest Bevin, who had been appointed in 1911 as a full-time official for the Bristol area of the dockers' union, became one of three national organisers of the NTWF in 1914. He was charged with preparing a scheme for a wider amalgamation of all transport unions. This plan was, however, delayed by the outbreak of World War One.

During this period before the war, unions organising miners, dockers and railway workers all staged strike action in Britain and Ireland. The 1911 Liverpool dock strike was particularly significant. Unusually it involved *all* transport unions (road, rail, port and sea), with Mann as chair of the joint strike committee. It generated mass solidarity action by workers in all industries, resulting in a local general strike which spread to many other ports around the country. This was a major challenge to capital and the state machine for which the latter, under orders from Churchill, sought to smash the workers with brutal retaliatory action. This culminated in an attack by police and soldiers on a mass meeting held on St George's

Plateau, Liverpool, in August 1911. Similar repression was meted out to striking miners from South Wales at Tonypandy in 1910.

In the summer of 1913, an industrial storm broke out in Dublin. The Irish Transport and General Workers' Union, led by James Connolly and Jim Larkin, took on the might of the Dublin employers. This signalled a general employers' offensive that led to 25,000 workers being locked out. The employers had no qualms about using the full might of the state to crush the Dublin workers; meetings were banned and workers arrested, including Larkin and Connolly. James Larkin had arrived in Ireland in 1907 as an organiser for the National Union of Dock Labourers (NUDL), the waterfront workers union. However, by 1908, disagreements with James Sexton, the leader of the Liverpool based NUDL, led to Larkin's suspension from the union, and so in 1909 he founded a Dublin-based union for unskilled workers – the Irish Transport and General Workers' Union (ITGWU) (no connection with the TGWU to be formed in Britain 13 years later). This was the union that led the strike initiated by Dublin tramway workers in 1913 which resulted in Larkin's arrest, excessive police brutality and a lockout of the strikers and their supporters. At least 15,000 workers were locked out because they refused to sign declarations rejecting the ITGWU. Thousands more, not on strike, faced destitution because of the knock-on effects of the dispute. They were all dependent on relief from outside sources, in particular from the Trades Union Congress (TUC) which raised roughly £100,000 for a hardship fund. A mass rally, organised by the *Daily Herald* in support of the locked-out Dublin workers, was held in London's Albert Hall in 1913. It was addressed, among others, by James Connolly and Sylvia Pankhurst. The significance of the rally was that it united the three movements – labour unrest, Irish nationalist movement and women's suffrage – which, separately and together, threatened the stability of the British ruling elite.

The TUC, however, failed to respond to calls from the ITGWU for sympathy strikes. Two union leaders in particular, J.H. Thomas (railwaymen) and Havelock Wilson (seamen) denounced Larkin's syndicalism and rejected any calls for supportive action. Robert Williams, as secretary of the NTWF, took a different view. He suggested that even if the TUC rejected sympathy strikes, it should at least call a special conference to discuss a boycott of goods from Dublin. This conference did indeed take place in December 1913. It made no decisions and as a result was criticised by Williams (who was excluded from the conference) as an exercise in futility in which personal rancour replaced political discernment.

Although most of the strikes in this period were defeated by repressive government action on behalf of employers' organisations, this did not deter trade union growth and extraordinary militancy. The Workers' Union membership grew rapidly, to around 500,000 by 1918 from 91,000 in 1914. The membership of the Miners' Federation of Great Britain

(MFGB) alone had leapt by almost 160,000 to over 900,000. The South Wales Miners' Federation, above all, gave practical form to syndicalist theory. In the wake of the defeat of the strike movement in the South Wales Coalfield 1910–11, syndicalist miners led by Noah Ablett set about reconstructing the union along the lines contained in a pamphlet widely discussed by rank-and-file miners and published in 1912 under the title *The Miners' Next Step*. This was the best and most popular expression of the syndicalist tradition. The South Wales miners' opposition to what they regarded as the encrusted and collaborationist MFGB leadership was matched only by their class hatred of the coal owners. The pamphlet advocated a wholesale repudiation of the existing system of conciliation and collective bargaining in favour of rank-and-file control of the union and workers' control of industry. To this end it proclaimed the syndicalist tenet: 'An industrial vote will affect the lives and happiness of workmen far more than a political vote [...] Hence it should be more sought after and its privileges more jealously guarded'.[6]

Syndicalism, however, was a mixed blessing especially for women. Whilst it captured the mood of and inspired the trade union militants of the pre-war years in a way that the small socialist sects failed to do, its appeal was nonetheless limited to the big industrial battalions from which women were largely excluded. Women were employed typically in 'sweated' trades or smaller industries, and as such, were bypassed by syndicalism. In any case, syndicalism's total focus on workplace struggles meant an explicit rejection of wider political issues, like the franchise for women – for which a massive campaign was fought at this time. Nonetheless, the syndicalist-inspired strike wave of this period helped to forge several amalgamations in the trade union field, especially on the railways and in transport. It also played a crucial role in the rise of the shop stewards' movement during the war years and the left-wing Minority Movement during the 1920s.

By 1914 it seemed as if Britain was heading for a social eruption. The combination of industrial militancy, the suffrage campaign and the explosive events in Ireland created enormous problems for the British state. For the government, the threats of imminent civil war (between nationalists and unionists in Ireland), militant class struggle and the radical women's franchise campaign seemed to suggest that Britain was on the brink of revolution. However, the outbreak of World War One in August 1914 earned British capitalism and its supportive state a temporary respite.

---

6 *Miners' Next Step'* (South Wales Miners Federation, 1912), p.2.

World War One and the Shop Stewards' Movement

War disrupts society. World War One was no exception, but far from disrupting the existing trends within the labour movement it had the effect of stimulating them. The militancy of labour's rank and file continued unabated, whilst the exigencies of war gave labour's leaders the chance to become fully enmeshed within the state apparatus. The gulf between the two widened to such an extent that it was difficult for both to co-exist within the same organisations. The 'unofficial' opposition, reflecting the chasm between leaders and led, generated its own structures in the form of the shop stewards movement and workers' committees. Although no longer unofficial, the shop stewards of today can trace their origins to this wartime period during which rank-and-file workers kept effective trade unionism alive in the face of their leaders' surrender.

British labour leaders, including Bevin and the leadership of the NTWF, maintained an anti-war stance up until the point, on 4 August 1914, that the government finally declared war on Germany. Thereafter, their opposition transformed itself not just into support but to wholesale co-operation in the war effort. By the end of August the Labour Party and the TUC declared an 'industrial truce' for the duration of the war and lent their support to an all-party recruitment campaign. Thus began in Lloyd George's words, 'a great new chapter in the history of labour in its relations with the state'.[7] This was supported by the leaders of all the transport unions, with the exception of one of the busmen's unions – the London and Provincial Union of Licensed Vehicle Worker (LPU) – the Red Button union. This union organised London cabdrivers and London bus and tram workers and it opposed the war from the outset.

Ken Fuller (historian of the London Busworkers) adds (in written comments on this chapter):

> While the LPU was anti-war, this was not without its problems. H. Bywater, the general secretary, and organising secretary Lawrence Russell both enlisted in the Army, leading to a bitter struggle within the union. Despite the fact that an annual conference decided that their positions should now be advertised, the Executive Council refused to implement this, and it was not until a conference in 1916 that the problem was resolved, with the EC forced to resign. It was during this period that a Vigilance Committee, largely rank-and-file but in which progressive officers like George Sanders (who felt free to act thus because he was elected instead of appointed) played a leading role. Why is this important? Because here we see the genesis of that progressive

---

7 Quoted in Davis, *Comrade or Brother?*, p.144.

tradition among London busworkers which led to the formation of a Rank and File Committee in the 1920s and the London Busmen's Rank and File Movement in the 1930s.

NTWF policy on the war was spelled out by its president (Harry Gosling) in his address to the federation's 1915 conference. He expressed what he thought was the view of the 'huge majority of our fellow countrymen' who are 'convinced that we are waging a justifiable war' in which the enemy must face us as 'an Empire, one and indivisible'. And so, 'with commendable restraint the trade union leaders counselled their members to remain at work'[8] and to reject any form of industrial action which might jeopardise the war effort.

By May 1915, there were three Labour MPs in the coalition government, one of them, Arthur Henderson, in the Cabinet. The two treasury agreements signed by government and trade union representatives confirmed labour's promise to abandon strike action for the duration of the war. It also drew the unions (including the ASE, whose members were principally affected) into agreeing to suspend 'restrictive practices' in skilled trades by agreeing to allow women workers, particularly in the war industries, to replace men recruited and in 1916 conscripted in the army. Similarly women replaced male workers in the road and rail transport industries. Despite now doing 'men's jobs', often replacing skilled workers, the women were almost always paid far less than the men they replaced. This was euphemistically known as 'dilution'.

Surprisingly, despite the ban on strikes and the willing compliance of the labour movement leadership, trade union membership increased by 17.5 per cent during the war. Among women, membership rose by 176.7 per cent between 1914 and 1918 (density rising from 8.0 to 15.9 per cent), so that a little under one in five trade unionists were female. The ban on industrial action meant that any wage increases during the war were only attained through compulsory overtime and bonus payments. But the cost of living, especially food prices, rose sharply during the war, hence real wages did not rise; a problem exacerbated by the 'patriotic' refusal of the NTWF and all unions to negotiate wage claims other than war bonuses. However, in 1915 the tripartite Committee on Production was established consisting of trade unions, government and employers. This clearly gave trade unions greater influence as well as introducing national pay awards in some industries. Key wartime industries like mining were effectively under state control during the war. Profiteering was rampant, thus nullifying the constant appeals to 'equality of sacrifice'. The NTWF was vocal in its opposition to the excessive profits made, in particular, by the shipping companies which capitalised on the war's reliance on their services.

8   Report of National Transport Workers Federation (NTWF) Fifth Annual General Council Meeting 1915 (Marx Memorial Library, hereafter MML).

The ambivalence of a section of the NTWF to the war was clearly apparent when conscription was introduced in 1916. It was the subject of a major debate at the NTWF annual conference in that year. A motion opposing conscription by the vehicle workers was supported by Bevin in which he singled out for special criticism Labour MPs for supporting conscription, and the military high command for their ineptitude in the conduct of the war. James Sexton and Ben Tillett both spoke against the motion opposing conscription. Tillett was a fervent supporter of World War One which he regarded as 'a people's war' and condemned those who opposed it as unpatriotic 'croakers'. The motion to oppose conscription was defeated.

Rank-and-file trade unionists in many industries, however, defied the leadership of the British labour movement's support for World War One and their backing for the government's ban on strikes. The role of elected workplace shop stewards was transformed during the war. They changed from being dues collectors to local negotiators, representing fellow workers in disputes with management. Thus shop stewards became an alternative trade union presence in the absence of the national leaders, absorbed as they were in fervent support for the war effort. A national network of shop stewards' committees was formed which became increasingly critical of the war itself. It was clear from 1915 that industrial workers were not going to be cowed by the legal strictures against strike action. An early example of this mood of defiance came from the strike by engineering workers in munitions factories in Scotland on the Clyde in 1915. The strike was, of course, unsupported by the leadership of the ASE. Aided by the hastily formed Central Labour Withholding Committee, the strike spread rapidly throughout the Clyde. Signs of mass defiance were not limited to Scotland. Even though some of these strikes were ultimately defeated, the organisation remained. On Clydeside, the Central Labour Withholding Committee was replaced by a permanent organisation – the Clyde Workers' Committee (CWC) – whose chairman, William Gallacher was a member of the British Socialist Party.

The CWC provided the model for similar organisations in other urban industrial centres. Its language was syndicalist, but its practice was not – in the sense that it sought to link the industrial struggle (based on the shop stewards) with wider community-based campaigns. The most famous example of this was the CWC's support for the successful Glasgow rent strike of 1915. Thus 'Red Clyde' was in the vanguard of the wartime workers' movement, but mass protests led by revolutionary socialists developed with as much force in other parts of the country. The election of shop stewards and the formation of shop stewards' committees was commonplace in most large factories which had been turned over to wartime production. In Sheffield, a workers' committee was formed on the model of the CWC. Other industrial centres like Manchester, London and later Birmingham also had workers' committees. Opposition to the war and socialist-inspired industrial militancy were greatly stimulated in 1917 with the news of the Russian Revolution. The October revolution probably did more than anything to challenge the syndicalist rejection of political involvement in favour of the notion that industrial struggle alone would lead to societal change. Russian workers and peasants had shown that revolutionary political action had resulted in the founding of a socialist state, something that strike action alone could not accomplish.

The Impact of the Russian Revolution

During World War One, Russia was an ally of Britain and France (the Triple Entente). Given that the leaderships of both the Labour Party and the TUC ardently supported the war, there was unease about the consequences of the Russian Revolution. Would it result in Russian withdrawal from the war? It was clear that the first revolution of February 1917 (Russian calendar) which overthrew the Tsar, did not pose a problem. The provisional government, headed by Prince Lvov and then Kerensky, supported the war. It was thus 'safe' to welcome this revolution. The Leeds convention of 3 June 1917, called by the ILP and the British Socialist Party (BSP), was impressive evidence of labour movement approval. It was attended by 1,150 delegates from a very broad range of organisations from centrist liberals, pro-war Labourites (for example, Ben Tillett and Ernest Bevin), leftists, pacifists, shop stewards and feminists (including Sylvia Pankhurst and Charlotte Despard). Clearly this was an indication that it was possible to win broad unity to oppose autocracy and to support replacing it with bourgeois democracy.

However, the second revolution in October 1917 elicited a much cooler response from the leadership of the labour movement. The first act of the new Soviet government was to withdraw from the war and negotiate a separate peace with Germany resulting in the 1918 Treaty of Brest Litovsk. Unsurprisingly, the official Labour movement leadership line was to oppose Soviet Russia's withdrawal from the war. As a consequence, the TUC and the Labour Party held aloof at this stage from either supporting the revolution or opposing allied intervention. In 1918 Britain and France, supported by 14 other countries, initiated war(s) of intervention against Soviet Russia. However, widespread support for the Bolshevik Revolution by socialists and militant trade unionists led to mass opposition to government policy. The Hands off Russia (HoR) movement campaigned for a general strike in order to force the British government to withdraw from Russia and to cease sending supplies and munitions to the counter revolutionaries (the Whites). The greatest success of the HoR was the refusal of the London dockers and coal heavers (NTWF affiliates) to load the *Jolly George*, a munitions ship bound for Poland. Bevin and the NTWF leadership officially supported their action. The consequence of the *Jolly*

George success was an intensification of the anti-intervention campaign which ultimately, by August 1920, drew in official Labour Party and TUC support.

A special conference, called by the TUC and the Labour Party, was held at the Albert Hall on 13 August 1920 to establish a Council of Action to oppose the escalation of the war against Soviet Russia. It warned the government 'that the whole industrial power of the organised workers will be used to defeat this war' and that the Council of Action 'will call for any & every form of withdrawal of labour' if the government does not back down.[9] This remarkable display of labour movement unity in support of a general strike succeeded in forcing the government to reverse its foreign policy – a singular triumph.

Ernest Bevin played a major role in this historic conference which was attended by over 1,000 delegates. He was a member of the National Council of Action and had led the deputation to the prime minister, Lloyd George, strongly opposing the government's anti-Soviet policy. Bevin's speech at the Albert Hall conference was fiery. In it he argued that demonstrations were not enough to stop war, and that 'the treatment meted out to Russia since the Revolution of 1917 was unparalleled in history of the world'.[10] Following the conference, over 400 local Councils of Action were established nationwide. The success of this initiative was summed up by George Lansbury, editor of the *Daily Herald*: 'I am sure the action taken by the Labour movement and the *Daily Herald* stopped the proposed British intervention. We were all united, all knew what we wanted, and were thus able to succeed'.[11] In short, in the face of the threat of a general strike, the government backed down.

Thus, pre- and post-war militancy, coupled with widespread support for the Russian Revolution, characterised this period. There were many strikes of a defensive character during the war, but 1919 witnessed the broadest and most serious strike wave yet seen. Thirty-five million working days were lost in strike action in 1919 – six times as many as in the previous year. This included strikes of those normally relied upon to carry out the repressive functions of the state – the police and the armed forces. Miners, transport workers and printers joined those who had been taking action throughout the war. Women were very involved in these strikes, particularly in the transport industry. The mood of this mass movement was influenced by the news of the workers' risings in Germany and Hungary and its strong support for the fledgling Soviet Russia. Unlike the wartime strikes, these, particularly the 1919 strikes in Scotland, were not defensive

9 The Council of Action, 'Report of the Special Conference on Labour & the Russian-Polish war in the Central Hall, Westminster, S.W., on Friday, August 13th, 1920'.

10 Ibid.

11 George Lansbury, *My Life* (Constable & Co., 1931), p.257.

– they were part of a political offensive against the power of capital and were all the stronger for their links with discharged soldiers and sailors.

Lloyd George cunningly held his Khaki election a month after the armistice was signed in 1918 and secured a massive victory for his coalition government. Labour won 60 seats but lost many of its more prominent MPs including Ramsay McDonald, Philip Snowden and Arthur Henderson. George Lansbury had lost his seat before the war and did not recover it in 1918. But peace with Germany did not betoken peace on the home front. The massive wave of militancy following the election shook the government. Such militancy provided the background for the febrile atmosphere in which the final process of amalgamation of transport unions was begun in 1920.

2

Creating the TGWU 1920–22

In which Ernest Bevin seeks to complete his plan for 'one big union'
for transport workers – but only partially succeeds

World War One and the temporary post-war boom had the inevitable effect of camouflaging the underlying chronic economic problems associated with Britain's loss of status as a prime manufacturing power. However, the post-war settlement, which divided German colonies between Britain and France, ensured that the British Empire increased in size to cover a quarter of the world's surface and population. Providing as it did a lucrative return on the export of capital, imperial expansion also served to mask Britain's manufacturing decline. This was a period of readjustment, economically and politically. The growing internationalisation of capital meant that Britain as a debtor nation could not fully control her own economic decisions. A new tension emerged between the interests of finance and industrial capital. Politically a new adjustment was necessary in the era of the mass franchise to accommodate a new two-party system brought about by the decline of the Liberal Party and its replacement by Labour as the main opponent of the Tories.

The Labour Party

In 1918, the Labour Party, in belated recognition of its official existence, adopted a socialist constitution and a programme. It also permitted individual members to join it as well as affiliated organisations, the most important of which were the trade unions which had founded its predecessor, the Labour Representation Committee in 1900. The new constitution adopted the famous socialist clause four which committed the party

To secure for the workers by hand or by brain the full fruits of their industry and the most equitable distribution thereof that may be possible, upon the basis of the common ownership of the means of production and the best obtainable system of popular administration and control of each industry and service.[1]

The other feature of the constitution was the introduction of a centralised method of electing the party's leadership at the annual conference on the basis of reserving seats for different categories of members. Five seats were allocated to local constituency organisations, four for women and the remaining 14 went to affiliated organisations; trade unions were by far the largest number in this category. As an affiliate, the NTWF and later the TGWU, soon to be Britain's biggest trade union, was destined to play a major role in the Labour Party. Trade unions now dominated the National Executive, resulting in a loss of influence of the socialist current, in particular via the ILP. Thus the ILP which had done so much to create the party was now marginalised and, as a consequence, the body it created lost the most active political guardian of its implied socialist conscience as reflected in its constitution. The fact that the constitution seemed so advanced is an indication of, and a tribute to, the revolutionary spirit which had engulfed the labour movement worldwide in the course and in the wake of World War One. Socialists, particularly those in the ILP, may well have been pleased that the party even came this far, at least in theory, but their hopes were soon to be dashed when it came to the acid test of Labour politics practically applied to concrete issues.

Post-war Economic Decline

The decline in Britain's staple industries was, after the war, an irreversible fact. The boost such industries had received under the impetus of the demand for munitions and uniforms during the war evaporated once the war was over. Coal, heavy engineering, shipbuilding, iron and steel, and textiles, the original foundations of Britain's industrial supremacy and already challenged by foreign competitors after 1870, paid the price for failure to respond adequately to this earlier challenge which was now compounded by the loss of export markets to old rivals and new ones in the form of Japan and the USA. British capitalism's failure to invest in the domestic economy exacerbated the problem. Thus it was, with all the built-in advantages of her greatly expanded Empire, British industry lagged sadly behind.

The continuing decline of the staple industries was in part responsible for the persistent high unemployment of the 1920s and 30s. Despite the

---

1   Clause 4, Labour Party Constitution, 1918.

fact that new industries began to develop, they were located mainly in the Midlands and the southern part of England, and did not compensate for, much less solve the problems, of the declining industries. Unemployment in the 'distressed areas' of the old industrial heartlands – South Wales, the west of Scotland, Lancashire, Tyneside and West Yorkshire – never fell below a million in the 1920s. But despite high rates of unemployment, trade union militancy increased. Such militancy centred on the mining industry, an industry which accounted for a sixth of the male labour force and was strongly unionised. The Triple Alliance, formed in 1914 by mine, railway and transport unions, was resurrected after the war and was activated in the 1920s in response to crises in the mining industry. Although the NTWF was part of the Triple Alliance, Bevin had long regarded the alliance as ineffective, viewing it as a 'shapeless mass', with 'no head and no direction'.[2] He thought the TUC would be better suited to co-ordinate action and thus he proposed that the TUC should establish a co-ordination subcommittee. This initiative led directly in 1921 to the establishment of the General Council as a replacement for the TUC's Parliamentary Committee. Bevin and Gosling played a major role in this reorganisation of the TUC. In 1919 Bevin's proposal for restructuring prefigured the outcome. His memorandum suggested that Congress should greatly develop and expand its industrial role alongside its political work. Thus he not only advocated the abolition of the Parliamentary Committee, but also proposed a radical structure for the new projected General Council. His suggestion was adopted in 1921 alongside a changed rule for delegate election to the new General Council. Until 1921 the basis for representation of elected members came via nomination from each individual trade union. Instead, Bevin's proposal was that the General Council should consist of eight industry-based economic sectors, later to be known as trade groups. This was very similar to the structure adopted by the TGWU in 1922 and is still used today by its successor union Unite: the TUC utilised it until 1983. It was abandoned thereafter for the still current practice of 'automaticity'; unions having a right to a prescribed number of seats on the General Council in proportion to the size of their membership.

Transport and the NTWF

Until 1920, the transport industry was largely unaffected by the adverse conditions affecting Britain's staple industries. World War One had given rise to major technological changes in transport, the most significant of which was the increasingly widespread use of motorised in place of horse-drawn

---

2 Quoted in K. Coates & T. Topham, *The Making of the Transport & General Workers Union*, vol.1, part 2 (Blackwell, 1991), p.754.

vehicles. In addition, the war had involuntarily encouraged national collective bargaining and trade union mergers. The wartime Committee on
Production, through its mandatory consultation with unions, had, by its
very existence, already unintentionally enhanced trade union power. Trade
union influence was further augmented in 1916 by means of the establishment of a government body for which Bevin had campaigned – the Ministry
of Labour. This new ministry had responsibilities for conciliation, labour
and industrial relations. It was established in order to act as a moderate
alternative to the shop stewards' movement's demand for workers' councils.
Influenced by the Russian revolution, militant trade unionists were inspired
by the revolutionary soviet system which had helped to create the new
Soviet Republic. Thus in 1918 the Ministry launched the Trade Boards Act
as a non- revolutionary alternative. This Act authorised the establishment of
Joint Industrial Councils (JICs), known in some areas as Whitley Councils.
These were joint union–employer consultative bodies with the aim of
reaching non-conflictual agreement on wages and conditions. They were to
operate in each industry on both a local and national level, thus requiring
inter-union co-operation within each industry. There were conflicting
opinions on JICs within the trade union movement. Some saw them as
vehicles for state incorporation, others like Bevin and Robert Williams
(secretary of the NTWF), took a more pragmatic approach. For them they
were a means of achieving a national organisation linking a wide range of
workers and hence encouraging teamwork between separate unions. They
also viewed JICs as a means of eradicating sweated labour. Indeed, great
stress was placed in the *Record*'s women's page on the importance of trade
boards for women in that they established a minimum wage in the female
dominated sweated trades. Seventy-four JICs were established by 1921, but
most collapsed in the late 1920s, other than those for white-collar workers.
Only those in the public sector in national and local government survived
beyond the 1940s. They were very short-lived in industries like coal mining
where there was sharp capital–labour conflict.

In addition to JIC's, sectoral union co-operation was given added
impetus by the 1917 Trade Union Amalgamation Act which now required
a simple majority for amalgamation based on a 50 per cent voting turnout
(previously it was two-thirds). This ushered in a spate of trade union
amalgamations after the war, the most significant of which was the
formation of the TGWU in 1922. Thus, trade union amalgamation was
given a boost, albeit unintended, by the economic needs of the state in,
during, and after WW1. Whilst not advocating the syndicalist 'one big
union' concept, trade unionists like Bevin were quick to take advantage
of these conditions to push for a more limited and pragmatic version of
amalgamation.

Bevin had long championed the amalgamation of transport unions.
One of the reasons for the prominent role he was to play in the amalgamation process of trade unions in the transport industry was attributable

to the national status he achieved in 1920 as a result of his role the Shaw Inquiry. This court of inquiry was established by Lloyd George's government, under the chairmanship of Lord Shaw, to investigate wages and working conditions in the docks. The NTWF chose Bevin to be its spokesperson for the dockers in the inquiry. As a former dock worker (he had been a carter at Bristol docks), Bevin's skilful advocacy on behalf of his fellow workers earned him praise from Lord Shaw himself and plaudits from the *Daily Herald* who dubbed him the 'Dockers KC'. A mass meeting at the Albert Hall was held in his honour at the close of the inquiry which had resulted in a successful outcome for dock workers. Casual labour was condemned, registration urged and a national minimum pay award of 16s per day for a 44-hour week was agreed. For Bevin this victory helped to reinforce his long-standing view that improvements in wages and conditions could be won through negotiation rather than strike action. However, strong resistance by the port employers ensured that the agreements reached were never fully implemented.

The Triple Alliance, the Miners and 'Black Friday'

The decline of Britain's staple industries was, we have seen, a prime cause of mass unemployment in the interwar years. The position of the workers who remained employed in such industries was grim. They were faced with a concerted attempt by the employers to cut wages and increase productivity. In 1921 British mines were handed back to the coal owners having been controlled by the government during WW1. The coal owners had failed to invest in the industry so now, in order to maintain their profits, they were determined to cut wages and increase productivity by lengthening the working day. Miners were thus at the centre of the employers' managerialist offensive. A defeat of the best organised trade unionists – the miners – would pave the way for maintaining profit in other industries by imposing lower pay and increasing productivity through labour intensification. The miners' union, the MFGB, demanded the nationalisation of the industry – a policy supported by the Sankey Commission. This Commission was appointed by the government in 1919 to avert a threatened strike for a 30 per cent pay increase. The Commission reported in favour (by a majority of one) of continued state control of the mines. Needless to say, the owners were vehemently opposed to any form of continued state intervention, let alone nationalisation. But Sankey played a crucial role in temporarily diffusing a potentially volatile situation. However, in the less revolutionary atmosphere of the 1920s, Lloyd George dropped all pretence at concession and in 1921 brought forward his plans to de-control the mines. This coincided (probably not accidentally) with the owners' announcement of savage wage cuts to well below pre-1914 levels and an ending of national wage agreements. The fact that employers in other industries were attempting similar tactics helps to account for the wave of support given by the labour movement to the miners when, as a result of their determined refusal to accept the demands of the mine owners, they went on strike and were then locked out.

In 1921, in accordance with its constitution, the Triple Alliance thus called a rail and transport strike in solidarity with the miners. As a member of the Triple Alliance, the NTWF now canvassed its federated unions to ascertain support for strike action. Only a third of these agreed to strike. Bevin himself was reluctant to back the strike, although Robert Williams, editor of the NTWF's influential *Weekly Record*, was more actively supportive. In Bevin's view the Triple Alliance was a 'paper alliance' and although it continued to hold meetings throughout the crisis, it did not receive a definite call from the MFGB for supportive strike action. Bevin said later that the miners' union had failed during this entire period to consult members of the Triple Alliance. He therefore concluded; 'if there is going to be unity in action there must be unity in counsel'.[3] Thus, after much vacillation, a conference of the Triple Alliance voted against solidarity strike action by a thumping majority – this included the NTWF delegates. The responsibility for this lack of consultation and indecision resulting in the Triple Alliance's apparent volte face was, however, mainly due to the backstage manoeuvring of some of the union leaders, notably Frank Hodges and J.H. Thomas (secretaries of the MFGB and the National Union of Railwaymen respectively). These two had held private talks with the government resulting, at the eleventh hour, in their decision to abandon the planned strike.[4] Bevin later said 'some of those who shouted the loudest [for strike] were the people who were damned glad that they were not called out'.[5] The miners, however, ignored the MFGB leadership's call to abandon the strike. They fought on alone through the summer of 1921 and were, after three months, starved back to work. They never forgave Hodges, who was replaced as MFGB secretary by a socialist and militant, A.J. Cook. Hodges was elected as an MP in 1923, serving as Civil Lord of the Admiralty in the 1924 minority Labour government.

3 Quoted in A. Bullock, *The Life & Times of Ernest Bevin*, I (William Heinemann, 1960) p.178.

4 London busworkers organised support for the expected miners' strike, combining with rank-and-filers from other unions to form the South East District Vigilance Committee and calling mass meetings for the night of 14–15 April. Furious at the last-minute betrayal, the Committee attracted 10,000 members to a protest meeting and then occupied the UVW head office. For a time it looked as if a breakaway might occur, as members at Merton, Old Kent Road and Nunhead garages withheld their contributions, but this was averted (Ken Fuller).

5 Bullock, *Life & Times of Ernest Bevin*, I, p.190.

The *Daily Herald* echoed the widely held view that the failure of the Triple Alliance and the decision of the leadership to call off the strike on Friday 15 April 1921 was a betrayal of the miners. Henceforth this event was dubbed 'Black Friday'. The *Herald* said it 'was the heaviest defeat that has befallen the Labour movement within the memory of man'. This view, expressed by the paper's editor, George Lansbury, was in sharp contrast to that of Bevin. Bevin was one of the directors of the *Herald* when, after the war, it had restarted as a daily paper, (during WW1 it had been a weekly). The *Herald* had always been short of funds and this was partly why Bevin was instrumental in handing the paper to the TUC in 1922. This decision, however, whether or not intended by Bevin, triggered Lansbury's resignation as editor.

The repercussions of Black Friday were keenly felt in the NTWF – many affiliates were critical of Bevin's role, as evidenced by the stormy NTWF General Council meeting in 1921. Fred Thompson, secretary of the London Dockers was at the forefront of the opposition to the NTWF leadership's position. Angered by such criticism, the council meeting served to confirm Bevin's view that the NTWF had outlived its usefulness. It gave added impetus and urgency to his aspiration to form an amalgamated union. Bevin justified his assessment thus: 'the present Industrial Situation [...] point[s] to the imperative necessity in the interests of the membership to create this new and powerful organisation at the earliest possible moment'.[6] The present 'industrial situation' to which Bevin referred was, as we have seen, that of the 1921 miners' strike and the ineffective role of the Triple Alliance.

After the miners were eventually starved into submission, they were forced back to work on far worse terms than they had before Black Friday. Their average pay fell by an average of 34 per cent. Their defeat led, as predicted, to lockouts to enforce wage reductions on engineers, cotton operatives, builders, shipyard workers, seamen and others. The newly formed Communist Party (CPGB) had a highly critical view of 'black' Friday which it regarded as a 'criminal betrayal of the miners'.[7] Robert Williams, secretary of the NTWF was also a member of the Communist Party, from which he was now expelled on the grounds that his federation had failed to support the miners.[8] In recent years, historians of the TGWU have countered the negative 'betrayer' verdict of Robert Williams by stressing the crucially important role that he played, both as secretary of the NTWF from 1912–21, and as a champion of the amalgamation

6 MRC MSS.126/EB/TG/1–2, Bevin Papers; minutes re amalgamation.

7 All quotations are from *Communist Review*, no. 1, 1921.

8 Interestingly the Home Office thought that Williams was 'working for the disruption of the Triple Alliance in the hope that RILU [Red International of Labour Unions]would sooner displace it' The National Archives (hereafter TNA) CAB 24/122/59.

of transport unions, inspired as it was by his unwavering socialist vision of 'one big union'. It has been argued that Williams could have been a potential leadership rival to Bevin had he not been discredited by the Communist Party in 1921. Instead he became the disgraced 'fall guy', unreasonably blamed, in part at least, for the Black Friday debacle. His declining influence was compounded by the fact that he lost his base as secretary of the NTWF itself in 1923 when the federation was wound up by the TGWU because in the view of the new leadership 'it serves no useful purpose in the present conditions of the transport industry'.[9]

However, the CPGB's condemnation of the betrayal of the miners and consequent expulsion of Williams contrasted sharply with its later contention that Black Friday was due to something much more fundamental than 'personal cowardice or treachery'. The Party argued that trade unionism had reached a new mass phase which meant that the industrial struggle to combat the power of capital must now reject sectional struggles and instead initiate mass strike action involving all unions. This was the policy of the Red International of Labour Unions (RILU) which had been formed by the Third (Communist) International in 1921 in the wake of the Russian Revolution and ensuing mass solidarity worldwide.

The Red International of Labour Unions (RILU)

According to Ellen Wilkinson, writing in *The Communist* in 1921, the RILU consisted of three main categories of trade unions internationally.[10] These, she identified, as a syndicalist group (French, Spanish and Italian unions), a Communist group represented by the Russians and thirdly, a centrist group consisting of the English and American trade unions. This centrist group, she argued, whilst they sought close connection between themselves and the communists, believed that 'revolutionary propaganda' in their unions would be more effective if it was 'undertaken by an industrial organisation clearly differentiated from the political party however close might be the working alliance'. This was clearly the policy of the British Bureau of the RILU which was established in 1921. Its first conference was chaired by Fred Thompson, secretary of the London District of the Dockers' Union (TGWU affiliate in 1922), a member of the Communist Party and RILU activist. The conference elected W. Gallacher and J.R. Campbell as joint secretaries and Tom Mann as chair. All three were communists.

---

9 MRC MSS. 625/1/1, Minutes & record of meetings of GEC & finance & emergency cttee 15 August 1923, minute 712.

10 Ellen Wilkinson was at that time a member of the Communist Party but was later, in 1924, elected as a Labour MP. She supported the 1926 General Strike and was one of the organisers of the Jarrow march in 1936.

From its inception the RILU had strong support within the trade union movement and especially among London dockers. Ben Tillett, in a letter to Thompson, complained that the latter had addressed a RILU meeting in his official capacity as district secretary of the London Dockers union.[11] Tillett was especially incensed that the London district had voted to disaffiliate, in favour of RILU, from the International Federation of Trade Unions (IFTU) – otherwise known as the Amsterdam International – to which the NTWF belonged. The TUC was affiliated to the IFTU and hence Bevin saw the RILU an anathema to the leadership of the entire British labour movement, particularly because the RILU was affiliated to the Third (Communist) International. As his personal papers indicate, Bevin showed a great interest in the RILU's operations and in Fred Thompson in particular. It was clear that Bevin was extremely concerned about the influence it was exercising in his own union and later in the TGWU. He described the RILU as 'contrary absolutely to our conception of democracy' – a phrase which encapsulated his hostility to what he regarded as a communist-dominated organisation. This opinion coloured Bevin's enduring anti-communist attitude throughout his tenure of office.

Amalgamation: The Process

The NTWF had debated the issue of amalgamation before WW1. At this time 58 unions existed in the transport industry. Indeed, the NTWF itself was the product of a federation of 15, mainly waterside, trade unions. The war delayed any progress to further amalgamation, but even after it, the dire economic and industrial situation seemed adverse. Nonetheless, Bevin continued to argue strongly for amalgamation and raised it again at the 1920 annual meeting of the NTWF. He was ably supported throughout by Robert Williams. At this meeting a schedule of other unions to be invited to an amalgamation committee was drawn up. By July 1920, a Joint Amalgamation Committee had been established with Bevin as its secretary and Harry Gosling, secretary of the Amalgamated Society of Watermen, Lightermen and Bargemen, as its chair. The agreed aim was to create a new union with a new name rather than fusing existing unions, thus giving a limited practical application to the idea of 'one big union'. For this to succeed the problem of creating unity while recognising diversity had to be solved. Bevin and his supporters achieved this by steering a route enabling the creation of a novel structure designed to protect occupational specificity national and locally while at the same time uniting them within a unified national and regional structure. This resulted in the formation of

---

11 MRC MSS.126/EB/X/37. The correspondence between Tillett and Thompson is preserved in Bevin's papers in a thick file labelled 'RILU'.

horizontal and vertical organisation comprising departments (later known as trade groups and now as industrial sectors) and 11 areas (later known as regions). Affiliation to the TUC and the Labour Party was accepted as a matter of course.

Many difficulties were raised in opposition to this proposed structure not least because existing unions would be absorbed into the trade groups. This would mean that the general secretaries of the merged unions would lose their positions. They were placated, temporarily at least, by the proposal that they could all act as assistant general secretaries during the period of transition. The trade group structure was designed to incorporate the many unions within each different broadly defined industry by cutting across traditional distinctions between unskilled, semi-skilled and skilled occupations. Bevin argued strongly at the monthly meetings of the amalgamation committee that the proposed structure had to reflect workers' shared economic associations within broad industrial groups covering a multitude of employers, rather than specific occupational or geographical connections. He won the argument against separatist particularism and it was agreed finally to create six trade groups: Docks Group, Waterways Group, Commercial Road Services Group, Passenger Service Group, General Workers Group and Administrative, Technical and Supervisory Group. These groups would comprise all workers within each industry, regardless of employer, with the promise to create additional groups as and when the union expanded. Each trade group was to have responsibility for policy making and conducting its own collective bargaining, with the caveat that strike action had to be approved by the General Executive Council (GEC). These national trade groups were complemented by corresponding counterparts in each region. However, these trade groups were not completely autonomous. They were unified at regional and national level by committees consisting of delegates from each trade group at regional and national level. This novel trade group structure – similar to Bevin's plan for the TUC General Council – subsequently attracted other unions to merge with the TGWU and in so doing the number of trade groups was expanded in later years. Industrial unionism (unions covering all workers in one industry regardless of job or skill), was not common in Britain. Craft unions existed as did general unions covering all workers regardless of industry. The name of this new union – the Transport and General Workers' Union, agreed by the amalgamation committee in 1920, reflected its hybrid character – hybrid, because it was both an (incomplete) industrial union and a general union, covering many trades, as well. Whereas its roots were in one industry (transport), it also expanded massively to cover workers in many other industries, including in 1929, the Workers' Union. This union, founded as a general union by Tom Mann in 1897, grew rapidly among women workers especially during WW1. By 1920 it had over half a million members covering a multitude of occupations and industries. However, its membership declined rapidly during the slump.

The ballot paper on the terms of amalgamation together with the rules embodying the new structure were sent to all participating unions inviting amendments. It was accompanied by a forthright and persuasive covering letter from Bevin in which he argued:

> Capital is well organised – every trade is interwoven and inter-linked. The great industries on the employers' side stand together! Labour must do likewise. [...] The scheme allows for the creation of a GREAT and POWERFUL UNION.[12]

With high rates of unemployment, a decline in trade union member-ship (by almost 1.75 million) and the defeat of the miners, circumstances were objectively unfavourable for the creation of a 'great and powerful union'. Nonetheless, during the three months of the ballot period, Bevin and his supporters led an unrelenting campaign in favour of amalgama-tion. Bevin alone addressed a vast number of large and small meetings, sometimes every day, under the slogan of 'One Big Union'. In August 1921, *The Weekly Record*, an NTWF paper, now became *The Record*, the monthly journal of the TGWU, and as such played an important role in supporting amalgamation.

Women Members

Despite the fact that the unions which were invited to ballot were almost exclusively male, *The Record*, from its inception in 1921 published a monthly women's page. This recognition that women were workers, and potential trade unionists, contrasted sharply with the proceedings of the newly formed TGWU. Once elected in 1922, its all-male GEC paid scant attention to women workers. Region 5 of the new union requested, on several occasions, the authority to appoint 'as an experiment' a temporary women's organiser.

Surprisingly this was rejected by the GEC, a contradictory position given that in 1922 the union had appointed two National Women's Officers – Mary Quaile and Mary Carlin. Mary Quaile had been an organiser for the Manchester and Salford trades council. She supported women's suffrage and was a member of the Women's Social and Political Union (WSPU). She had backed the pro-war faction of the WSPU when the movement (and the Pankhurst family) split in 1914. She was one of two women elected to the General Council of the TUC in 1924 and was part of a trade union delegation to the Soviet Union in 1925. Mary Carlin was the first woman to become a national officer of the NUDL. When this union amalgamated with the TGWU, she became its joint National

---

12 Quoted in A. Murray, *The T&G Story* (Lawrence & Wishart, 2008), p.36.

Women's Officer. Carlin was elected to the National Executive Council of the Labour Party in 1924. However, despite the appointment of women's officers at a national level, the early editions of *The Record* were characterised by the predominant chauvinist culture of the labour movement of the 1920s. For example, in its Christmas issue of 1921, 'Our Women's Page' noted that 'we women folk will be looking around for gifts for our dear ones'. Noting that money was a problem, helpful instructions were given on how to make a 'golliwog' as a suitable home-made gift. As time went on the content of the women's page improved, especially as the union began to recognise the need to recruit more women members.

Amalgamation: The Result

The success of the amalgamation campaign resulted in a three-day conference in Leamington in September 1921 to approve the draft rules to which over 200 amendments had been received. The conference was attended by 140 lay delegates (all male) representing the trade unions which, at this stage, had voted in favour of amalgamation. Bevin reported on the progress of negotiations with other unions and explained that the unfavourable economic climate had meant that the amalgamation scheme could not be extended as widely as he would have desired. It was, however, clear at Leamington that despite the spirit of organisational unity, major disagreements of a political and personal nature persisted. Bevin was challenged in the election for general secretary of the new union. It was a three-way contest – his main opponent was the secretary of the London Dockers, Fred Thompson, a communist, and, as we have seen, a stern critic of the Black Friday betrayal. Thompson's election address was a foretaste of the subsequent revolt of the London Dockers against the industrial strategy of the new union. His candidacy, was, in his words:

> a challenge to autocracy and a protest against the building up of a new Union around individuals instead of policy. The present industrial situation demands a new orientation of the functions and purposes of the trade union movement, together with a definite programme.[13]

Bevin won the election comfortably with 96,842 votes. This was ten times more than Thompson, who was his nearest rival. Harry Gosling was returned unopposed as President of the TGWU, a post in which he remained, without facing a contest, unelected, until he retired in 1930. Ben Tillett (still General Secretary of DWRGLU, the union formed

13 TGWU *Record*, December 1921.

after the 1889 dock strike), was expected to stand as president. Gosling would have stood down in favour of Tillett, but Bevin persuaded Tillett to withdraw on the (possibly spurious) grounds that 'it would put the amalgamation at risk'.[14] It is possible that Bevin thought that because he and Tillett had been members of the same union, it would be unacceptable for both to hold the two most senior posts in the new union. Nonetheless, it was clear that there was personal animosity between the two men and whatever the reason, Tillett reluctantly stood down. As a result of Bevin's opposition to his candidacy, Tillett opined that 'some of my worst suspicions have been fully justified'.[15] Later he wrote an angry letter objecting to the lack of a full published report of the Leamington conference.[16] Tillett added that 'already there is too much suspicion of intrigue and self-seeking abroad, which will mitigate against the harmony which induces efficiency and relieves the mind of suspicion of autocratic domination'.[17] So, although the outcome of Leamington was successful, it was certainly not harmonious.

By the time that the TGWU proudly announced its official existence on 1 January 1922, 14 unions had delivered a majority vote of the necessary 50 per cent legal turnout and were thus part of the amalgamation which now totalled 300,000 members. However, two dock unions, James Sexton's NUDL and the Scottish Dockers and Stevedores polled well under 50 per cent. By the end of the year, six more trade unions had joined. Although the United Vehicle Workers (UVW) voted to amalgamate, it was clear that there was opposition to the decision especially among many branches of London Busworkers. London busmen, even though they were members of the UVW, continued to express doubts about the merger leading to serious concerns that they would secede from the TGWU. More than 20 London bus branches called for a special conference.[18]

Bevin and Gosling were alarmed enough to head off this threat by convening a special conference themselves to which three delegates from each London bus branch were invited. The conference was duly held in December 1921, the result of which was the establishment of a London Bus sub-section within the Road Transport Trade Group. Hence London Busworkers acquired a unique and special position within the TGWU, with their own elected officials and their own conference. Although this solved the immediate threat of a breakaway, it also created a powerful,

---

14 Quoted in Coates & Topham, *The Making of the Transport & General Workers Union*, vol.1, part 2, p.844.

15 Ibid.

16 He was especially irked because there was no mention of the complaint registered by the National Union of Dock Labourers (NUDL) against Bevin for touring the country and allegedly poaching members.

17 MRC MSS.126/TG/42/4/2/2.

18 Ibid.

Region 1

*What was the reason for London UVW Busworkers' hostility
to the merger with the TGWU?
Why did Bevin agree to establish the London Bus sub-section?*

George Sanders expressed misgivings about the amalgamation because a) the National Union of Railwaymen (NUR) and Associated Society of Locomotive Engineers and Firemen (ASLEF) were not included and b) 'the officials of some of the Unions that we are asked to amalgamate with went over to the side of the capitalist class while the late war was in progress' and 'there is no guarantee that in a crisis they would not do exactly the same again, and as the majority of the members of these Unions probably acquiesced in their attitude, it is a point that must be looked at'.

More broadly, until 1920 London busworkers had been members of a relatively small, tightly-organised union, the LPU, in which they had been able, often after a struggle, to ensure that their full-time leaders were accountable to lay democracy. In addition, they were prone to strike in order to impose their will on employers; they could obviously see that this freedom might be threatened if permission to strike had now to be sought from a more remote GEC of the TGWU. Aside from the principle of lay democracy, they feared that their previous practice of electing *all* full-time officers might now be threatened – as, indeed, it eventually was. For two years, they had existed within a previous amalgamation, the UVW, in which some of these principles had already been tested.

It was for these reasons – and fears of a breakaway – that Bevin was forced to agree to the creation of a London Bus Section, with its own Central Bus Committee, which had immediate access to the general secretary (Ken Fuller).

militant and well-organised group which laid the foundation for future opposition and unofficial action. London busmen were to become an enduring thorn in Bevin's side.

In April 1922 elections were held for the new GEC. This was to consist of one representative from each of the union's 11 areas and one representative from each of the six trade groups. All had to be lay members. The GEC would henceforth meet quarterly for five days in London. The great disappointment was that two important sectors of the transport industry – sea and rail – held aloof from amalgamation. The two rail unions, ASLEF and the NUR retained their independence as did the National Sailors' and Firemen's Union (NSFU). George Sanders, a full-time official of the UVW, wrote in the UVW *Record* that without the two rail unions 'an amalgamation of transport unions is not complete'.[19] An additional setback for the TGWU was that another general union was formed in 1924. This was the National Union of General and Municipal Workers, the successor to the Gasworkers' and General Union, formed as a result of the Great Dock Strike of 1889. Thus, ironically, two competing general amalgamated unions had emerged from the unified struggle which had heralded the birth of new unionism 35 years previously.

---

19 Quoted in Ken Fuller, *Radical Aristocrats: London Busworkers 1880s to 1980s* (Lawrence & Wishart, 1985), p.65.

3

The TGWU and the Labour Movement 1922–24

Which sees Bevin confront the left, survive two unofficial strikes and then challenge Britain's first Labour government

Introduction

The TGWU was formed at a time when Britain was faced with major economic problems and important political and industrial changes. Mass unemployment helped to account for a fall in trade union membership by 1922. But a decline in membership did not betoken a decline in militancy. Strike action was almost as prevalent as hitherto – in 1922 alone there were almost 20,000 strikes and strike activity continued, culminating in the biggest display of working-class mass mobilisation yet seen – the General Strike of 1926. However, the vibrancy of the movement cannot be measured simply by the number of strikes. Other indices include the existence and viability of a range of organisations capable of giving expression to working-class aspirations inside and outside the workplace. Several such organisations were particularly significant in this period. The RILU has already been mentioned. It continued to exercise an important influence in the trade union movement. Poplarism was another influential movement. This was the campaign, begun in the London borough of Poplar, led by George Lansbury, to defend living standards in working-class areas by insisting that the domestic rate should be used for local purposes. The movement to organise and draw attention to the plight of the unemployed, the National Unemployed Workers' (Committee) Movement (NUW(C)M), led by Wal Hannington and Lillian Thring, was very active in the 1920s and 30s. In addition in some areas, particularly in compact mining villages, trade unionism and community politics fused to produce a revolutionary outlook in such a singular fashion that these places earned the nickname of 'little Moscows'.

The fact that a minority Labour government took office in this period could also be said to be an indication of a more general political belligerency, but the experience of Labour in office only served to underline the continued need for extra-parliamentary organisation, as shown by the organisations briefly mentioned above. At local and national level the rank-and file movement from 'below' indicated once again the fissure between leaders and led, or more accurately, between left and right. The influence of the Communist Party in most of the mass campaigns in the interwar period had the effect of politicising such protests, but at the same time sharpened the divisions between left and right. Divisions had always existed, but the fact that Labour became a party of government made its cautious leaders especially anxious to gain the approval of the establishment by presenting a cautious and respectable face. The state machine saw the Soviet Union and hence communism as its main enemy. Labour was thus determined to distance itself from this 'taint'. The leadership of the labour movement managed to regroup itself after it had lost ground as a result the mass struggles during and immediately following WW1. Given the leadership's continued commitment to reformist politics, it was unlikely to learn the lessons the left was anxious to teach it. Rather, it attempted to strengthen its grip on the movement and in doing so helped, alongside the more powerful vested interests of capital, to reduce the influence of the socialist left. It is in this context, of the struggle between left and right, that the early years of the TGWU must be analysed.

Amalgamation and the Political Environment

The Communist Party of Great Britain
In the heady atmosphere in the wake of the Russian Revolution and continued post-war militancy, the talk of communist unity became at once more urgent and more realistic. Attempts had been made to unite the disparate socialist parties and factions during the war on the initiative of the BSP, but it was not until after the war that any real headway was made. The minimum condition for participation in the post-war unity talks was an acceptance of Marxist theory. Agreement on theory (and in theory) proved to be much easier than agreement on strategy and tactics. The talks in 1919 and 1920 revealed deep disagreements on two major questions – whether or not to affiliate to the Labour Party and whether or not to participate in local and parliamentary elections. The intervention, by letter, of Lenin in these debates certainly helped the less sectarian position to triumph, even though it failed to convince some of its supporters like Sylvia Pankhurst of the Workers' Socialist Federation. In August 1920, the Communist Party of Great Britain was founded. It was, and for many years remained, tiny. Its influence, however, was

immeasurably greater than the sum total of its membership. From the very beginning it had within its ranks the leading industrial militants who had led the massive pre-war strikes and who had formed the core of the shop stewards' movement during the war. To these were added, either in 1920 or later, other individuals and small groups who had either been 'converted' to Marxism or induced to jettison pure syndicalism because of the war and the Russian Revolution. The South Wales Socialist Society, a descendant of the pre-war Miners' Reform Movement and some of the Guild Socialists (like R. Page Arnot, Ellen Wilkinson and Walter Holmes), fell into this latter category. A left-wing group within the ILP, including such individuals as Shapurji Saklatvala, R.Palme Dutt, Emile Burns and Helen Crawfurd, may be counted among the former.

It would be wrong to lay any false claims about the significance of the formation of the Communist Party (CP) in 1920 given the stranglehold of the by now well entrenched reformist and labourist traditions in Britain. Equally, however, it would be wrong to deny the importance of the Communist Party's existence. For at least 60 years it was the only significant Marxist organisation in Britain providing a focus for the activities of the left, politically and industrially. As such it was a force with which the ruling class and the right-wing labour leadership had constantly to reckon. It was clear from the outset that close watch was kept on its activities. Special Branch reported regularly to the Home Secretary on 'revolutionary organisations in the United Kingdom'.[1] These included reports on various organisations thought to be causing trouble to the state at different times, but CP activity was constantly monitored. The reports, marked 'secret', were presented to meetings of the Cabinet and clearly indicate that at this time the CP had an impact on the labour movement out of all proportion to its small membership. The government was so alarmed by the influence of this, as yet very small party, that in May 1921 it ordered a raid on the CP's London headquarters at 16 King Street. The office was ransacked and the general secretary, Albert Inkpin was arrested on charges of sedition under the terms of the notorious Defence of the Realm Act (DORA), introduced to enforce patriotic compliance during the war. Inkpin was sentenced to six months' hard labour. Willie Gallacher, former secretary of the Clyde Workers Committee and now the party's organiser, was also arrested. The RILU's offices were similarly raided and ransacked. The secret service reports also indicated that the CP was playing a leading role in organising unemployed workers, many of whom were ex-soldiers. In 1921 the Party had founded the National Unemployed Workers' Committee Movement (NUW(C)M). It sought, with varying degrees of success, to organise among the unemployed and campaigned for the next 25 years under the slogan of 'Work or Full Maintenance'. It

---

1 *The Record*, July 1924.

was responsible for the use of daring and innovative methods of protest including hunger marches, factory raids to protest against overtime working and mass demonstrations often aimed in particular at Poor Law Guardians who were still responsible for the administration of poor relief under the archaic provisions of the 1834 Poor Law Amendment Act. Women played a prominent role in the Movement. Lillian Thring was the editor of the NUWM paper, *Out of Work* and from the outset a place was reserved on the National Administrative Council for a women's organiser. Barely a year after the foundation of the CP, Special Branch reports indicated that communists were also having a significant influence in trade unions and industrial disputes.[2] In particular it was noted that through the RILU, communists were gaining the support of the miners and London dockers.

The First Labour Government 1924
One of the first decisions made by the TGWU was to affiliate to the Labour Party and as one of the largest affiliated unions, it exercised a powerful influence. The Labour Party increased its representation in the House of Commons in the General Elections of 1922 and 1923 (142 and 191 seats respectively). This included eight TGWU members, six of whom were returned with financial support from the union. No-one, including Ramsay MacDonald, who had been re-elected as Party leader, expected that he would become prime minister in 1924. The Tories were in disarray over the issue which had historically divided them – tariff reform. Unable to unite his party and with no overall majority in parliament, their leader, Baldwin dissolved it, leaving Labour as the next largest party free to form a government provided it obtained Liberal support – such were the formal (and unfavourable) circumstances in which the minority Labour government of 1924 came into being. Tariff reform, whilst a problem for the Tories, was but a fig leaf to cover a more sinister manoeuvre. In a situation of high and rising unemployment, and without a policy to alleviate it, the Tories were genuinely concerned that it would only be a matter of time before a majority Labour government was elected. Such a government, if its 1918 manifesto was to be taken seriously, would pose a serious threat to the owners of wealth. Asquith, the Liberal Party leader, agreed with Baldwin. For the Liberals, a Labour government 'with its claws cut' was infinitely better than one which was truly independent. This explains why the Liberals did not, as was in their power, help save the Tory government and instead threw in their lot, for nine months, to prop up, while it suited them, this first Labour government. (It was also the case that the Liberals, as traditional free traders,

2 TNA CAB 24.

could not in any event support the Tory policy of Protection – masquerading under the euphemism of tariff reform).

The establishment parties showed undue alarm at the prospects of Labour's radicalism, let alone its socialism. Although dependent on Liberal votes, this was not a coalition government, hence the fact that Ramsay MacDonald went outside the ranks of his own party to find cabinet ministers was a matter of some concern to the Labour rank and file. He selected Lord Haldane, a former Liberal minister, as Lord President and the posts of Lord Chancellor and First Lord of the Admiralty went to two Conservatives (Lords Parmoor and Chelmsford respectively). Labour Party members in the Cabinet included two prominent trade unionists, Harry Gosling (TGWU) and J.H. Thomas (NUR). Those trade unionists including J.R. Clynes, Thomas and Margaret Bondfield who were appointed to the Cabinet were required to relinquish their seats on the TUC General Council. They were replaced by left-wingers, George Hicks, A.J. Swales and A.A. Purcell.

Further evidence for the groundlessness of the fears of the establishment was to be found in the Labour government's attitude to the rising wave of strikes. It elevated its hostility to them almost to a point of principle. MacDonald, a captive of Treasury orthodoxy, was as concerned as his predecessor, Baldwin, about trade union militancy. Baldwin had revived and remodelled the strike – breaking machinery established during the war. This took the form of the innocuously named Supply and Transport Committee (STC). The Labour government not only retained the STC but strengthened it with the inclusion of notable labour movement figures including Sidney Webb, Arthur Henderson and an experienced trade unionist, J.H. Thomas. The STC was utilised in 1924 to combat two TGWU official strikes – a national dock strike and a strike of London tramway workers. Bevin was summoned to the STC to discuss these strikes, but was unwilling to co-operate. The dock strike was settled but Bevin complained of the threats emanating from the parliamentary leaders of the Labour Party, who justified their anti-union stance by claiming to be acting in 'the national interest' – putting 'country before party'. Such threats were made real during the strike of London's transport workers when the government went to the lengths of invoking the hated Emergency Powers Act. This Act, passed in 1920, enabled the government, by declaring a state of emergency, to break any strike which prevented 'the supply and distribution of food, water, fuel or light, or with the means of locomotion'. On this occasion, the force of the Act was not activated only because the strike was settled. However, Labour's anti-strike stance led to a permanent rift between Bevin and MacDonald. Despite this, the TGWU's opinion of Labour's relationship with trade unions was unexpectedly mild. *The Record* commented that the union was 'aware of the government's difficulties, but a policy of industrial truce would not be in the best interests of the Government [...] governments may come and governments may go, but the workers fight for the betterment of conditions must go on all the time'.[3]

It is surprising, given the extent of the Labour government's hostility to mass action, that the establishment went to the lengths it did to discredit Labour. This came in the form of the infamous 'Zinoviev Letter' - the publication of which was a classic example of establishment conspiracy and cost Labour, as intended, the 1924 general election. Although the government could have been toppled at any time, the issue which finally settled its demise was the Campbell case. J.R. Campbell, acting editor of the communist *Workers' Weekly*, published the famous 'Don't Strike' open letter to the army urging them not to act as strike-breakers. For this he was charged under the 1797 Incitement to Mutiny Act, but when the charge was dropped the government was held responsible and lost a vote of censure in the Commons. Three days before the ensuing general election, a letter purporting to come from the Communist International organisation, signed by its president, Zinoviev, was leaked by the Foreign Office to the press and published in the staunch Tory paper, the *Daily Mail*. In it, the promise of 'Moscow gold' was made to finance armed insurrection in Britain and although the letter was addressed to the Communist Party, the fact that it alluded to the draft treaties on trade and co-operation between Britain and the Soviet Union. which had been negotiated by MacDonald's government, meant that a connection was supposed to be made between the Labour Party and communism. The fact that the letter was an obvious forgery and that anyone who was seriously concerned with the truth could not believe for one moment that MacDonald had any sympathies with communism, did nothing to prevent the 'red bogey' distorting reality and doing the sinister job for which it was intended. The Tories obtained a comfortable majority in the 1924 general election. Six TGWU members were elected with union financial support and two other members were elected, without financial backing. This included John Scurr – a socialist – elected as MP for Mile End. Ben Tillett, however, lost his North Salford seat.

Women Workers

Although *The Record* published a monthly women's page, the TGWU was a male-dominated union, with an all-male GEC. Its first annual report contained one of the very few references to women workers in this period of the union's history.[4] It noted that women had been hit hardest by the attack on wages especially in industries not covered by trade boards, resulting in their having 'been forced back to absolutely sweated conditions' (report's

---

3 'Labour's Industrial Policy' *The Record*, April 1924.
4 MRC MSS.126/TG/1154/1, 31 December 1922.

emphasis). Somewhat portentously it stated that male members had not done enough to retain and fight for better pay for women members. It warned that the 'lower the standard to which these workers are reduced the greater the danger to the male workers and the whole community' (report's emphasis). *The Record* reflected that the 'organisation of women is uphill work at the moment' and that '[s]ince the amalgamation the women's section has been somewhat overshadowed in the turmoil of settling down into our gigantic stride'.[5] It called on male members to recruit their wives and daughters and stated that the two national women's officers, Miss Quaile and Miss Carlin, would offer assistance in any area.

Women members were congratulated on their role in the 1924 general election. *The Record* stated that women were integral to Labour victory. However, this was not a political compliment. Rather women were praised because in the absence of committee rooms, 'without a word of complaint' women had allowed their front rooms to be used during the election campaign. This, 'great sacrifice' on their part was at the expense of domesticity since 'the pride a woman takes in her little parlour is well known'. Their homes were turned 'upside down', but when the campaign was over, the women 'worked with a will to restore order' in their domestic realm. However, at the same time as extolling women's traditional domestic role, the journal also began to seriously champion the recruitment of women members, although its appeals were restricted to 'Our Women's Page', a page which may not have been read by male members. Perhaps this accounts for the fact that in March 1924 the first of several graphic bold notices appeared on the back page of *The Record* (not on the women's page), headed 'An appeal to our men in all sections'. It went on, 'may we remind you that the TGWU is a union for both sexes' and 'unity is strength; solidarity means men and women standing shoulder to shoulder'. Again the assistance of Miss Quaile and Miss Carlin was offered. The TGWU was represented at the first biennial conference of the International Federation of Women Workers, held in 1923. It was reported there that the total women's trade union membership in Britain was 832,000. (It was over double this number in Germany.) The TUC was clearly concerned about the low level of women's membership, regarding it as an urgent matter at its 1923 Congress. It exhorted affiliates to remedy the situation, stating that recruitment could be improved 'if all trade unionists would do their utmost to get their wives and daughters to see the importance of becoming trade unionists themselves'.[6] The TGWU supported this approach, but warned against rivalry between different unions attempting to recruit women workers at workplace level. By May 1924 *The Record* reported that women's membership was increasing, not because men were

5 Our women's page, *The Record*, October 1923.
6 *The Record*, July 1924.

actively recruiting their wives and daughters, but because 'women are beginning to realise that they have many things they might have retained had they been loyal to themselves and remained organised'. This seems to suggest that women themselves were the problem. The journal was not a fan of feminism. In an article supporting equal pay for equal work, it opined that 'the sentimental slush of the feminist' is not responsible for the demand for equal pay and that the 'average woman' remains unconvinced by feminist arguments and their supposed support for the 'sex-war'. In contrast the TGWU argued that progress could only be made if men and women worked together. However, once again women themselves were in part held responsible for their super-exploitation. It was claimed that 'women are cheap today not because their work is inferior but because they have not yet realised the value of organisation'.[7]

The TGWU and Industrial Problems

In comparison to the relatively smooth process of amalgamation, the early years of the TGWU were stormy. The 1922 annual report noted that it was difficult to give accurate membership figures due to the slump-induced decline in membership. In addition, the report noted the grave discontent among members due to the continued fall in wages, resulting in 'a spirit of abject fatalism [...] creeping over the whole movement'.[8] *The Record*, commenting on the first quarter of the TGWU's existence explained that 'as soon as new union started, there was launched upon nearly every section we represented, employers trying to force down wages far below trade agreements'. However, the militancy of the times did not demonstrate 'abject fatalism'. This was reflected in Bevin's closing sentence in which he condemned the Baldwin government as clearly representing 'great industrial and financial interests' which 'make it impossible for the workers ever to be divided again by the cry of Liberalism or Toryism. Now, it is clearly Capitalism versus Labour'.[9]

Docks
Despite the TGWU's reported membership increase of 35,000 in 1923, 'a very big revolt of a section of the membership'[10] rocked the equilibrium of the union. Starting in Hull, an unofficial dock strike took place in most major docks including London, Bristol, Birkenhead, Cardiff and Manchester. The port employers sought to impose a wage cut of 2s a day and an extension

---

7   *The Record*, July 1924.
8   MRC MSS.126/TG/1154/1. First Annual Report, 31 December 1922.
9   Ibid.
10 MRC MSS.126/TG/1154/2. Second Annual Report, 1923.

Dock Strikes

Dave Penn

(Region 1)

The 1923 United Kingdom dock strike started in June 1923, when over 50,000 dockers were unhappy about a proposed pay reduction of 8 shillings to 5 shillings and 6d, which in today's money would be a reduction of 40p to 25½p for a four-hour minimum working period. The general secretary at the time – Ernest Bevin of the newly formed Transport and General Workers Union – had signed an agreement with the bosses without informing the members of this agreement. The strike started in Hull and spread to the whole of the UK. Through this agreement, made behind closed doors, thousands of dockers left the TGWU to join the Amalgamated Stevedores Labour Protection League. This union then formed the National Amalgamated Stevedores, Lightermen, Waterman and Dockers Union, which after a while became the National Amalgamated Stevedores and Dockers Union (NASDU), of which I was a member up until 1982 when I joined the TGWU through amalgamation of the two unions. Before the 1992 amalgamation, the Lightermen and Waterman joined the TGWU. The strike lasted for eight weeks after which the dockers were forced back to work through hunger etc. The reason for it was an unofficial dispute was because the general secretary of the union signed the agreement without the members knowing.

1924 Official Dock Strike Review

In 1924 work conditions for dockworkers were generally very poor. They were usually employed on a casual basis, day by day, and had little if any job security. There was often competition between gangs of dockers which sometimes could break into violence. In Liverpool, for example, there were teams of Scottish, Irish, Welsh and Manx dockers, and employers would use this rivalry between the dockers to keep wages low. A strike was called in February 1924 when relations between employers and employees reached breaking point. The following statement comes from a meeting of government officials.

> The Minister of Labour informed the Cabinet that following the breakdown of direct communications between the parties involved in the Docks Dispute, he had invited a joint meeting of employers and employees to take place at the Ministry of Labour at 2.30 the same day. He proposed to open the meeting with a few words, after which everything would be done to explore the possibilities of settlement. (CAB 23/47. C12 (24)4 National Archives)

This dispute started on 12 February and lasted until 21/22 February. This was followed by another statement from the Minister of Labour, which read as follows:

The Minister of Labour made a full statement to the Cabinet, regarding the settlement of the dispute, which he hoped would lead to a resolution, there were certain terms that were on offer to the unions, such as an increase of wages of 1/- (5p) per day at once and a second 1/- (5p) on the first Monday in June and remission of the decasualisation to a committee of employers and employees and that was intended to be a real settlement in the Docks Industry. It only remained for the representatives to the TGWU who had their Executive Committee behind them to consult the Delegate Meeting, and the results of the consultation ought to be known by 7pm the same evening. (CAB23/47 C16 (24)2 National Archives, 21 February 1924)

This dispute seems to be handled better by the union, unlike the previous dispute in 1923 when the general secretary made an agreement without consulting members.

of the working day by one hour. The union rejected this and accused the employers of reneging on the letter and spirit of the 1920 Shaw Inquiry. Nonetheless, negotiations continued with the union's national leadership, and a compromise settlement was reached, the terms of which were to be agreed by the membership. The agreement retained the current eight-hour working day, but in return agreed to the wage reduction but that it should be spread over two years (1s in 1923 and another 1s in 1924). A national agreement was signed to this effect. The trade union side justified this compromise at a national delegate conference in which Bevin reasoned that 'if trade revived it would be easier to win back the money than it would be to shorten the hours of labour once they had been extended'.[11] Thus, so the argument went, in the current economic climate a choice had to made between either maintaining wages or sacrificing conditions. However, despite the support of the National Docks Group, this national agreement did not win the support of the mass of the membership. Sixty thousand dockers went on unofficial strike in most of the major docks, but without official support the strike petered out except in London where it was strongly supported by the mass of dockers and the East End community. Bevin and the TGWU leadership opposed the unofficial strike as 'a serious revolt against the National Agreement', denouncing its unofficial leaders and especially the communists of wishing to destroy the union. These unofficial leaders

11 *The Record*, August 1923.

were accused of feeding the strikers with 'a daily diet of lies'. Bevin and Gosling were howled down at a mass meeting of 2,000 London dockers at Bermondsey Town Hall. They were accused of being 'traitors and blacklegs'. This incident was condemned in *The Record* as 'probably the most despicable in the annals of trade union history'.[12] The strike on the London docks continued after dockers in other ports had reluctantly returned to work. Eventually, after seven weeks, the London strike committee's recommendation for a return to work was accepted but not without opposition, which led to the stevedores splitting from the TGWU. They formed a breakaway union, the National Amalgamated Stevedores, Lightermen, Watermen and Dockers Union. This union, formerly the Stevedores' Labour Protection League (a TGWU affiliate) had recruited TGWU members during the dispute. This was serious enough for the TGWU to refer the issue to the TUC disputes committee. The new stevedores union was found guilty by the TUC and was ordered to return the members they had 'poached' to the TGWU. There were additional problems for the TGWU in Hull where the Workers' Union (WU) was accused by the TGWU of 'the most unscrupulous behaviour that any national union could possibly be capable of'.[13] The WU was accused of poaching TGWU members in Hull during the unofficial dock strike. Again the TGWU referred the matter to the TUC disputes committee. Although the TUC found against the WU, it did not rule that it should cease organising in the docks.

However, the affront to the TGWU's leadership caused by the unofficial London dock strike was not laid to rest. Bevin, greatly angered, initiated an investigation. His papers contain a very thick file devoted entirely to it, labelled the 'Thompson Inquiry'. Clearly, Bevin saw his old adversary, Fred Thompson, secretary of the London dockers, as the villain of the piece. He was specifically named by Bevin as a CP member and activist in the RILU. As a result, instigated by Bevin, the GEC carried out a special investigation which reported in December 1923.[14] The inquiry blamed 'outside organisations' for inciting the dispute. It named the Communist Party in particular. Referring to the CP, the GEC report said that whilst CP members were free to join the TGWU, the union 'cannot retain in their employment any officer who would be pledged to receive instruction from an outside body on matters [...] affecting the Union'.[15] This was clearly a reference to Thompson. The inquiry claimed that the strike was not a genuine upsurge of rank-and-file dockers. Rather it had been organised by officials who were both misusing their position by acting on instructions from an outside organisation, as well as misusing the property of the

12 *The Record*, September 1923.
13 MRC MSS.126/TG/1154/2. Second Annual Report, 1923.
14 MRC Bevin papers: Report & executive decision regarding matters arising prior to and during the unofficial dock strike, 21 November 1923.
15 Ibid.

union as a base for RILU activity, in this case the Poplar office (Newby Place). Hence the inquiry stipulated that in future the offices of the union must only be used for 'legitimate union business' and no 'outside body' should be allowed to participate in union affairs. Furthermore it ruled that henceforth the union's area secretaries should play a much more prominent role in co-ordinating the work of all the trade groups within their area and that they should convene meetings of all group secretaries at least once a fortnight. This decision was clearly influenced by the highly critical 'statement on the Dock Dispute' by J.T. Scoulding, the Area no. 1 secretary who published a two page report in *The Record* (September 1923) in which he detailed what he described as 'the disgraceful tactics' of the London leaders of the unofficial strike.

Buses and Trams

Before amalgamation there had been more than eight unions involved in passenger road transport, the largest being the UVW, a militant union which had been opposed to the Black Friday betrayal of the miners in 1919, and although sceptical about amalgamation, had joined nonetheless. In London in 1923, busmen who already had their own special status in the TGWU took action when the employers, the London General Omnibus Company (LGOC), proposed a wage cut. Members of the bus section voted overwhelmingly against it. As a result, faced with such opposition, the LGOC withdrew their proposal. In a further show of strength, the London busmen held a rally of 10,000 men at the Albert Hall in February to protest against proposed wage reductions and receive a report of the negotiations from Bevin. According to Bullock, 'over the next 20 years London busmen were to give Bevin more trouble than any other group in the union'.[16]

As we have seen, the two official strikes of 1924 on the docks and London tramways were opposed by the minority Labour government. These two strikes were given full union support because by the end of 1923, a temporary economic recovery appeared to present an opportunity to reverse the pattern of wage reductions of the past three years. The Dock Group submitted a claim for a pay increase of 2s per day and some of the safeguards agreed by the Shaw Inquiry, but had not been honoured by the employers. True to form, the dock employers rejected the claim in January 1924, coinciding, possibly deliberately, with a Labour government about to take office. The following month all dockers nationwide struck. It was the strength of this strike, undaunted by government intimidation, which prompted the employers to concede.

The second official strike in 1924 by London's tramway workers was in response to the employers' proposal to reduce wages by 5s per week.

16 Bullock, *Life & Times of Ernest Bevin*, I, p.XX.

LONDON TRAM AND BUS WORKERS ON STRIKE.

One of the few remaining buses. A crowd besieging a Shep-
herd's Bush bus in Piccadilly-circus yesterday afternoon.

'An informal conference at Putney. A wounded
"Tommy" wants to know why 'he has to walk.

Figure 1: London Tram and Bus Workers on Strike

Credit: *Past Tense: London Radical Histories and Possibilities*

The 1924 London Tramway Workers Official Strike and Solidarity Strike Action by London Bus and Underground Workers

Joanne Harris

To understand the reasoning behind the tram workers strike action of 1924 it is important to understand some of the background leading to this point. Throughout 1921 and into 1922, bus workers' terms and conditions were under attack because of the economic situation building in the country. The tram workers were even less fortunate and between October 1922 and October 1923 they had lost five shillings per week in wage cuts. A court of inquiry in 1921 had recommended standardisation of wages but nothing had come of it. In 1923 further cuts were announced by the three main private tram operating companies because of the increasing competition from motor buses.

In 1922 many 'pirate' bus operators appeared on London's streets, there was little regulation at the time and competition was fierce. By 1924 an estimated 500 independent buses were operating on London's streets together with the large operating companies like the LGOC. Most independent operators only had one or two buses in their 'fleet' and they all operated on the busiest of routes and at peak times. Competition was so fierce that buses would kick their passengers off before the end of the route if it looked more profitable to turn round and go the other way. Buses would cut in front of the bus in front to get the lion's share of passengers and sometimes fights would break out between the bus drivers.

To sort out these pirate companies the Transport & General Workers Union (T&GWU) was putting enormous pressure on the government to form a single traffic authority which would govern the bus operators and put an end to the madness. This wasn't the first time this had been attempted as the single traffic authority had been called for by a select committee in 1919 and a Royal Commission in 1905, but nothing had come of it.

The huge growth of these independent companies impacted heavily on the tram companies who were struggling to maintain their passenger base and were suffering financially. In June 1923 the three tram companies operating in London proposed cutting the wages of tram workers by five shillings per week. The TGWU countered on 3 December with a wage increase demand of eight shillings per week.

It is important to understand that whilst bus and tram workers were mostly governed by the same people and had the same union there was an enormous pay disparity between them. At the time bus workers were on 86s 6d per week whilst the tram workers only made 67s per week. Bus drivers would get to full wages within six months whilst tram drivers took two years to achieve top money for the job.

On 24 February 1924 a mass meeting of tram workers held at Wembley stadium was called and over 10,000 attended, being bussed in from every corner of London. The tram workers instructed their committee to announce a strike on 15 March if no agreement was met. Immediately the bus workers announced a sympathy strike action for the same day. Both actions met with approval of the T&GWU under Ernest Bevin.

Harry Gosling who was the President of the T&GWU and minister of transport in the newly elected Labour Party asked for calm and the strike to be delayed until further talks could be had. This was unanimously put down by the workers.

The two sides met on 20 March at the Ministry of Labour and despite both private companies the LGOC and LCC offering arbitration and a court of enquiry being ordered at midnight, that same night the strike began.

By the next day 16,000 tram workers were on strike together with 23,000 bus workers in their solidarity action. This put enormous pressure on the underground and remaining 300 pirate buses. Three days later the underground workers announced their intention to join the solidarity action with the tram workers.

The government under pressure rushed through the London Traffic Act of 1924. The bill got its first reading on 25 March and on the 28 March the strike was called off.

The London Traffic Act 1924 got royal assent on 7 August 1924.

> The act imposed restrictions on who could operate buses and the routes they could travel, which regulated the amount of buses on London's roads and on who could actually ply their trade. This in turn practically killed off the competition overnight. The main operating companies bought out most of the 'pirate' operating companies. The trams had won a valuable reprise and on the back of the successful action the T&GWU gained many new members, but Bevin went on to score an own goal when he later refused to back a bus worker strike in that same year, but that is another story…

Sixteen thousand tram workers struck in March supported by solidarity strikes by London underground workers and London busworkers. Again the Labour government showed its hostility, this time invoking the hated Emergency Powers Act. This intimidation did not deter the union. A compromise agreement with the employers was accepted by ballot and the strike was settled.

Although the TGWU supported and settled two strikes in 1924, this did not signify serenity in the union. Its third annual report welcomed the growth in membership, following a period of falling growth.[17] Thus the report asserted that the amalgamation was a great success, indicating that the TGWU had, in practice, shown that it 'has been possible […] to combine craft unionism and the occupational interest'. This was echoed in *The Record* which argued that recent events had demonstrated the power of 'one big union' and had vindicated 'the group and trade committee system'. The efficient organisation of the union had brought for the members 'greater benefits than the more spectacular display of strikes'.[18] However, a significant caveat to both this and the report's optimism was Bevin's assertion that 'there is a section of our movement who, whilst […] preaching unity, take advantage of every opportunity to carry on a propaganda which is purely of a disruptive character'.[19]

Clearly, Bevin was referring to the support for the RILU, in particular in London, and its effective descendant, the National Minority Movement (NMM), formed in 1924. The aim of the NMM was to give 'organised expression to the progressive minorities in all working-class organisations. There being such minorities in political and cooperative working-class organisations, as well as in the trade unions'.[20] Bevin was as implacably opposed to the NMM as he was to the RILU. He regarded the NMM

17 MRC MSS.126/TG/1154/3. Third Annual Report, 1924.
18 *The Record*, January 1924.
19 MRC MSS.126/TG/1154/3. Third Annual Report, 1924.
20 The National Minority Movement, 'What the Minority Movement Stands For' (1924), https://www.marxists.org/history/international/comintern/sections/britain/subject/minority/nmm.htm.

The 1924 London Busworkers' Affiliation to RILU and the Impact it had on the TGWU Leadership

Joanne Harris

The RILU was an organisation created by the Communist International to forward its aims of co-ordinating communist activities within trade unions. Established in 1921 the RILU, or Profintern as it was sometimes called, was intended to act as a counterweight to the Social Democratic IFTU which was an organisation branded as collaborationists and an impediment to revolution by the Communist Party.

The RILU focused its attention on the unions of Great Britain, and their chief, Mikhail Tomsky, travelled to England in 1924 followed by a reciprocal visit by a high-level delegation of the TUC headed up by A.A. Purcell. This laid the groundwork for many similar visits back and forth to forge ties between the Soviet and Western trade unions. RILU began to organise within the bus workers and that organisation became known as the National Minority Movement (NMM).

The TGWU's first general secretary, Ernest Bevin (1922–40) was quite a conservative right-wing leader who was opposed to communism and direct action, and although he supported the earlier tram worker strikes in March 1924, he opposed the bus workers taking action over wages and conditions later in the same year. Bevin never really supported any strikes in the whole term of his leadership.

Following much negotiation, the RILU, under the name of National Minority Movement (NMM), was formed in August 1924 and at its inauguration attracted 271 affiliates. The movement was at its strongest in London and whilst records are pretty scarce it would appear that the bus worker NMM strength was centred around North London garages such as Holloway, as that garage was instrumental in the threatened strikes over schedules by nine garages in early 1925 whilst strikes took place in Plumstead and Sidcup. The British trade union leaders had little interest in the RILU and saw them as a sham or nuisance, but the British delegates came out openly in favour of the Russian unions thus causing a rift. After the General Strike the gap between the NMM and the TGWU widened even further, to where at one stage it would seem that a split was on the cards. The famed early newsletter and first edition of the *Busman's Punch* was probably written and edited by the NMM's, George Renshaw.

as an organisation which claimed 'the right to interfere with the majority executive councils and even [to interfere with] ... himself as General Secretary'.[21] NMM was particularly well supported by London busmen, but it was clear from Bevin's personal papers that for him it exercised an unwanted influence in the union as a whole for the following five years at least. His enduring complaint was that the NMM represented a rival pole of authority to the TGWU organisationally and politically. He put it thus 'the more we grow in power, the more some people think we can be used for some policy or other outside our organisation'.[22] His view was that the average worker only wants decent wages and that this can be obtained within the capitalist system.

For Bevin the strength and unity of trade unionism nationally was the only way to secure improvement in workers' wages and conditions. To achieve these ends a strong central national leadership was essential. This was Bevin's strategic vision in the creation and the organisation of the TGWU. The two successful official strikes of 1924 indicated the merits of the centralised organisational structure of the union. However, this centralist imperative was not without its critics, especially among the socialist left often condemned it (and Bevin) as authoritarian. The tension between the leadership of the TGWU and the unofficial movement inside and outside the union thus characterised the early years of amalgamation.

21 MRC MSS/126/EB/MM/1.
22 Ibid.

II

From Challenge to Collaboration
1925–28

Introduction

Section I has focused on Bevin's achievement in creating the TGWU. As we have seen, Bevin did so in the most difficult of conditions, i.e. mass unemployment and an anti-union employer offensive. He was able to do so by concluding deals with major firms in industries that were relatively sheltered and not dependent on export markets: bus, tram and commercial transport, flour milling, the docks, industrial chemicals and food processing. All were relatively vulnerable to strike action. All saw the benefits of long-term recognition deals. This strategy did enable Bevin to consolidate the TGWU, although it brought conflict with those in the union who carried forward the militant politics of the immediate post-war years, as earlier chapters have detailed.

However, still in 1925 Bevin considered himself a socialist in fairly immediate terms. He wanted to see basic industries taken into public ownership and saw a Labour government as the necessary vehicle. He also believed, at this stage, that the extra-parliamentary strength of the trade union movement would be essential in carrying forward this process. In 1920 he had chaired the TUC Committee of Action that threatened a general strike to halt war with Soviet Russia. In 1925 and again in 1926 he backed general strike action in support of the miners.

By 1927–28 Bevin had revised his views. He no longer saw general strike action as constitutionally legitimate, and socialism no longer as an immediate prospect. Instead he was involved, along with other trade union leaders, in discussions with employers about modernising the British economy and doing so within an empire-based trading system. For the defenders of the existing order and the opponents of socialism, Bevin's change of position was seen as a major strategic gain – in some ways the biggest of the interwar period.

Bevin held a central position in the Labour movement. He controlled the country's dominant union, was paymaster of the Labour Party and ran the party's daily paper. His new alignment, and that of the TGWU, decisively shifted the balance.

Speaking privately to fellow Conservatives in the Athenaeum Club in 1938, former Tory prime minister Stanley Baldwin claimed that his greatest political achievement had been to educate the British Labour Movement in constitutional government. As a result, he said, Labour had accepted that industrial action must never again be used to put pressure on an elected government. This change of position, and Bevin's part in it, will be the focus of Section II. Bevin's political shift affected much that followed in history of the union: the relationship with the 1929 Labour government and the role of the TGWU during the war and the subsequent decade. In fact, the union would only only regain its progressive momentum under Frank Cousins in the later 1950s.

The period 1924–27 should therefore remind us that in writing the history of any union it is vital to pay attention to the actions of the 'other side', the representatives of the employing class. Their interactions with the representatives of labour will often be of critical importance. For this period we will have to consider them in some detail. In doing so it is important to remember that those who represent employers, and 'capital' in general, are never a monolithic block. They had different personal objectives, different backgrounds and often pursued different strategies – though all were united by the commitment to maintain the existing order.

The central figure was Stanley Baldwin himself, leader of the Conservative Party since 1922. His family firm, Richard Thomas and Baldwins, was one of Britain's biggest steel-makers. He was related to both Rudyard Kipling, the empire poet and the pre-Raphaelite artist Edward Burne-Jones, and liked to portray himself as above the partisan positions of his fellow Conservatives, a 'one nation' Tory. Bevin came to hate him more than any other Conservative. He had good reason.

A close ally in government was the Minister of Labour, Arthur Steel-Maitland, from a Scottish coal-owning and landed gentry family. He was the main go-between with trade union leaders – assisted by Sir Horace Wilson, permanent secretary at the Ministry, a key figure in the 1914–18 wartime management of the trade union movement and later an architect, with Baldwin and Chamberlain, of appeasement policies with Nazi Germany.

In the Cabinet there were two members of the Cecil family, a family involved in government since the period of Elizabeth I. The Marquis of Salisbury was an empire loyalist and supported a policy of direct confrontation with Labour and the trade union movement and tended to align himself with Churchill. His brother Robert Cecil liked to portray himself as more liberal, a proponent of the League of Nations who had sought to create a united party of Conservatives and Liberals to oppose Labour.

Winston Churchill, member of another long-standing 'governmental' family, had moved politically from the Conservatives to the Liberals and back again to the Conservatives. He was seen as unduly ambitious and prone to reckless adventures. As a Liberal cabinet minister he was notorious for his use of troops against strikers. After returning to the Conservative Party Baldwin brought him into the Cabinet as Chancellor of the Exchequer with the remit of returning the pound to the gold standard at 1914 parity with the dollar – a politically hazardous task which meant, as Baldwin said, that 'all wages must come down'. Churchill favoured direct confrontation with the trade union movement – and in this was supported by F.E. Smith, Lord Birkenhead, Lord Chancellor in the post-1924 government and previously an outspoken supporter of Ulster Loyalism and the Curragh mutiny.

Not in the government but a key adviser was the Scottish industrialist Lord Weir. He was president of the National Confederation of Employers' Associations. He had been a wartime government adviser and President of the Air Council. He was a director of Shell, ICI and Mond Nickel and had close ties with the City, especially with Lord Kindersley, a director of Lazards and of the Bank of England.

Another key figure was Alfred Mond, later Lord Melchet, managing director of Brunner Mond chemicals (later ICI), previously a Liberal cabinet minister who joined the Conservatives in 1926. He controlled a significant section of the monopolised growth sector of the economy in electrical engineering, motors (Lucas) and industrial chemicals. Brunner Mond was one of the first firms with which Bevin concluded a recognition deal. Brunner Mond/ICI rented one floor of the TGWU head office in the 1920s.

4

Preparations for the General Strike 1925–26

In which the government prepares to tame the labour movement and teach it a lesson about unconstitutional action

The first minority Labour government lost office in November 1924 when the Liberals, who previously gave them support, withdrew. They did so in order to vote for a Conservative motion of censure against the Labour Attorney General. As the government's legal officer, he had halted prosecution of the editor of the Communist *Workers Weekly* for publishing an article calling on troops to refuse deployment in industrial disputes.

The decision to oust Labour from government reflected a more general unease in the political establishment. While Labour's exercise of government was intended to strengthen the authority of the party's constitutionalist right wing under MacDonald, and had to an extent done so, it was felt by the autumn of 1924 that Labour was drifting dangerously in the other direction. There was concern at the Labour government's decision to start negotiating a trade treaty with the USSR. Worse, it was felt that the Labour leadership was not standing up to the Left in the trade unions and constituencies at a time when communists still remained full individual members of the Labour Party. This had been starkly illustrated by the decisions taken by TUC in September 1924. The congress had given new powers to the General Council to call a general strike, had welcomed the leader of the Soviet trade union movement and voted through a workers charter calling for the nationalisation of land, minerals, mines and railways, an extension of state enterprises and a 44-hour week.[1]

---

1 Earlier in the year, clear indication of state-level concerns about Left influence are apparent from the actions of the right-wing Home Secretary, J.R. Clynes. Using material supplied by the security services, he had raised with the Cabinet the growth in communist and Minority Movement influence in the trade union movement, and

Rank-and-file Militancy and the Return to the Gold Standard

These worries about growing Left influence were made especially acute by the impending return to the gold standard at its pre-war parity with the dollar – overvaluing it by up to 10 per cent. This return to the gold standard had been a prime objective of British policy since the end of the war and was seen as essential if the City of London was to be restored as the prime international banking centre. Ramsay MacDonald himself, in his capacity as foreign secretary, had helped smooth the way by securing support agreements with the French. But everyone knew that one key consequence of the gold standard would be heavy competitive pressure on exporting industries, coal particularly. Prices – and wages – would have to come down. Hence, the last thing needed was a revival of the kind of politicised rank-and-file radicalism seen just four years before in the immediate aftermath of the war. The influence of the Left within the labour movement would have to be curbed and if the Labour leadership was incapable of doing this, then the Tories would have to do so themselves.

The conduct of the election gave vivid illustration to these concerns and the need to drive a wedge between Labour's 'constitutional' and 'unconstitutional' wings. Baldwin and the Conservatives issued a manifesto stressing the need for 'social peace' and a government that would listen 'to all sections'.[2] Yet just before the election, the Foreign Office and intelligence services connived in the production of a forged letter in the name of the secretary of Communist International, Zinoviev. In it Zinoviev was represented as instructing the Communist Party to prepare for armed insurrection. Ramsay MacDonald himself, as outgoing prime minister and foreign secretary, gave credence to the letter. In doing so he further underlined the wider political message that was taken up by the press: the communists and their Left allies in the Labour Party and the trade union movement were bent on destruction – but people of good will, both those at the helm of the Labour Party and those leading the Conservatives, could work together for the common good. The election saw the Liberal vote collapse as middle-class voters deserted to the Conservatives. As a result Labour lost seats. But the Labour vote itself rose massively. Despite the Zinoviev letter, the Labour support jumped from 4.2 to 5.2 million. Tory concerns intensified.

After the election, in his 1925 New Year message to TGWU members, Bevin struck a strongly optimistic note. 'We are satisfied of this, however,

sought to involve trade union leaders in direct cooperation with the security services to combat it. Cabinet agreed that details of left-wingers should, in strict confidence, from now on be passed directly by MI5 to appropriate trade union leaders: TNA Cab 24 166/73: J.R. Clynes, 'Industrial Unrest', 31 April 1924.

2 Bullock, *Life & Times of Ernest Bevin*, I, p.265.

that the Movement will not swing back to the Right; it will swing further to the Left' and in a strong criticism of Ramsay MacDonald and Snowden, 'in our view there can never be an adulterated Labour government in this country again'.

He continued: 'the year that has passed was a wonderful year for this organisation and indeed for the whole movement. At its opening developments were going on which had within them the potentialities of either making or breaking this organisation'. He mentions the unofficial movements of 1923 but 'the loyalty of members could not be broken'. He then highlights the 'two huge struggles' of 1924, the dockers' movement and the passenger workers movement, from which the union had emerged 'successful and strengthened'.[3] However, he also warned that the Conservatives were planning an attack on the movement, specifically on the political levy, to weaken the Labour Party and its links with the trade unions.

What Bevin did not mention at this stage was the government's preparation for the gold standard and its implications for wages. Baldwin had appointed Churchill as Chancellor with a remit for an immediate return to the gold standard. Wages would have to come down for all export staples. Churchill announced the return in his April 1925 Budget and six weeks later the coal owners, responsible for the country's biggest export industry, gave notice that they would end existing agreements on wages and hours on 31 July. This set the fuse for the biggest industrial conflict in the twentieth century, the 1926 general strike.

Red Friday: The Government Retreats

Immediately, in July 1925, the battle appeared to turn in favour of the miners and the trade union movement. Carrying forward initiatives at the TUC from the previous year, the TGWU, along with the NUR, ASLEF, the Engineers and a number of smaller transport unions had formed a 'Quadruple Alliance'. In this Bevin and the TGWU had a key role. The TGWU was the first union to formally endorse the alliance at its biennial conference in Scarborough in June 1925. It was also the union that had the best potential for bringing the country to a standstill – from the docks, to the buses, trams, road haulage and canals. 'This', Bevin wrote the following month, 'acted as a great stimulus to the miners and gave a general lead to the movement The absolute willingness of that great conference to place the whole Union at the disposal of the General Council [TUC] was a demonstration of solidarity it is good to have lived to see' – even though Bevin went on to warn 'it is too early to shout complete victory'.[4] Faced

3 *The Record*, January 1925.
4 *The Record*, August 1925.

with the Quadruple Alliance and the threat of general strike action from the TUC, the government offered a wage subsidy to the mine owners for the following nine months and agreed to appoint a Royal Commission to examine the economics of the coal industry. It made this announcement on the day the mine owners' ultimatum expired on Friday 31 July – quickly named Red Friday in contrast to Black Friday in 1921.

Some ministers at the time, and some historians since, have claimed that this retreat was because the government's emergency arrangements were not ready. Those close to Baldwin saw the issue in a different light. For them the ground had not been prepared *ideologically*. They worried that a major conflict, or an overt legal attack on the Labour movement, would push the great mass of trade union members back towards the more revolutionary perspectives of the immediate post-war period. For this reason, in early March 1926, Baldwin had squashed a call from the Tory right wing to outlaw the trade union membership levy for the Labour Party. In doing so he made his famous declaration that the government stood for 'peace in our time'. It was not the government that would embark on class war.[5] Further time was needed to drive a wedge between the centre of the trade union movement, represented by Bevin, and what was seen as the 'unconstitutional' Left.

The dangers of precipitate action had been summed up by one of Baldwin's main allies – the Minister of Labour Steel-Maitland – in a cabinet paper written in mid-May 1925. Maitland examined wider political trends in the trade union movement, arguing that that the previous Triple Alliance had failed because it was between union leaders and not rooted in the membership.[6] He feared the Quadruple Alliance was different. 'The Minority Movement appears to be actively supporting the projected alliance if indeed it did not inspire it. A number of the more active members of local branches in all the unions concerned belong to this movement.' He continued that there was 'deep seated discontent among large sections of rank and file' and the danger of this 'bubbling over into a widespread dispute'.[7] In 1921 the government won because it had been able to manipulate differences between union leaders. Now, he argued, rank-and-file unity, and a level of political mobilisation at the base, would make this much more difficult. A couple of weeks later the Home Secretary, the hard-line Joynson-Hicks, also raised issues of potential political discontent within the police – asking for more money for police pay, referring to the 'serious discontent' that existed in 1919 and noting

5 K. Middlemas in *Politics of Industrial Society* (André Deutsch, 1979), p.126 makes these points based on the papers of Lord Davidson, in 1925 Chancellor of the Duchy of Lancaster and a close adviser to Baldwin. The Colonial Secretary Leo Amery as well as Steel Maitland took similar positions.

6 TNA CAB 24 172/41. Steel-Maitland, 18 May 1925.

7 Ibid.

that the police were 'unsettled' and the Police Federation was demanding a reversal of previous cuts.[8]

An Ideological Offensive Against the Left

The government's subsequent ideological offensive had two fronts. One was to isolate Communist Party influence at a time when communists were still members of the Labour Party (and in London made up a significant section of the membership) and, in the main, were simply identified as those who, as members of the Labour-affiliated BSP, had organised the wartime shop stewards' movement against right-wing pro-war union leaderships.. The other front was related but politically more fundamental. It was to redefine the permissible limits of trade union action. The trade unions had to be taught that it was not constitutionally legitimate to use strike action to bring pressure on an elected government. In both these objectives Baldwin thought he could rely on active support from the right wing in the Labour Party leadership gathered round MacDonald, Snowden and J.H. Thomas.

Bevin himself held a position that to some extent cut across these lines of attack. He had fought his own battles with the radical Left just 18 months before in the docks, buses and trams and saw its defeat as central to his vision for the union. Yet he also believed in the organised strength of the trade union movement and its right to rectify social injustice by bringing pressure to bear on governments including the use of general strike action. At the biennial conference in July 1925 he challenged the Labour right-wingers on this: 'I could say a word also to my Labour friends who are always raising the constitutional issue. It won't be raised by those of us who have to lead the strike. The question of the form of government in this country will not come within the purview at all. The question that will arise is justice for the men who have given their lives in industry'.[9]

Bevin presented himself above all as an organiser, believing that the Labour movement's unity and strength had to be protected if it was to be collectively used for social justice in the political arena. But he did not go much further. In a speech some months later in Glasgow, where the TGWU was in dispute with the trades council over its affiliation to the Minority Movement, he argued: 'he did not want Minority Movements or Majority Movements but a Great Working Class Movement [...]. Capitalism had failed as a system and would eventually destroy itself'.[10]

8 TNA CAB 24 173/91. Joynson-Hicks, 12 June 1925.
9 MRC MS 126/TG/1887/1. Report of the First Biennial 1925.
10 TGWU *Record*, April 1926.

The first stage of the attack on the Left came in September at the 1925 TUC. On the surface it might appear that the Left was victorious. Chaired by the left-winger Alonzo Swales of the Engineers, it had reasserted the demand for a trade treaty with Soviet Russia as providing the markets needed to tackle unemployment. It had applauded Tomsky as representative of the Soviet trade unions, passed a motion in support of a call for the use of industrial action for political ends – including the establishment of workers committees capable of taking power – and condemned the Labour government's participation in the Dawes Plan, a key step towards the restoration of the gold standard.

But on the crucial issue of preparation to defend the miners, the block votes of the NUR and the TGWU were used to deflect plans for action. The miners moved that the General Council be given more powers to organise united strike action. J.R. Thomas tried and failed to secure outright rejection. Bevin, however, careful not to be identified with the Right, had moved a successful amendment that the issue be referred back to the General Council. Organisationally also there were also important changes to the composition of the General Council that strengthened the Right and Centre. J.R. Thomas and Margaret Bondfield, previous Labour cabinet ministers, became members along with Bevin himself. The right-wing steelworkers leader, Arthur Pugh, became chair. And within three weeks the left-wing General Council secretary, Fred Bramley, unexpectedly died and was replaced by his assistant secretary, Walter Citrine.

Then in October at the Labour Party's conference, the right wing in the Labour Party launched its own attack. This was to isolate the communists ideologically within the Labour Party. At this stage it did not attempt to exclude communists from membership but to prevent them standing as Labour MPs – as had been the case with Walton Newbold and Shapurji Saklatvala, MPs for Motherwell and Battersea respectively. The attack was led by Thomas and MacDonald. Bevin, on behalf the TGWU, gave his support although in a qualified fashion: 'if he thought this was a move to expel the Left Wing or attempt to stifle criticism, he would have to oppose it' but communists could not 'conscientiously reconcile' their beliefs with the Labour Party's political perspectives.[11]

Within days of this motion being passed the government itself intervened – amid a fanfare of press coverage that revived all the fears of the Zinoviev letter and violent revolution. In two successive raids on the Communist headquarters in early October, 12 members of the leadership were arrested. They were charged under the Incitement to Mutiny Act of 1797. The government prosecutor made clear that the charge against them was not their socialist opinions but their commitment to the violent overthrow of the country's constitution and that they sought to do so on

---

11 TGWU *Record*, October 1925.

behalf of an alien power. They were, in the words of the sentencing judge, 'members of an illegal party carrying on illegal work in this country'. In the dock Harry Pollitt warned that the 'government sought to remove from the political arena the most effective exponents of united action by the working class to aid the miners'.[12] He went on to attack the associated newspaper campaign. The trial was eventually concluded in November with sentences ranging from six months to a year.

The Government Prepares – The TUC Does Not

Citrine's diaries, as incoming General Secretary of the TUC, reflect the confusion and conflicting pressures of the following months.[13] The General Council did not discuss the mining issue at all, delegating it to a subcommittee, the Special Industrial Committee (of which Bevin was not a member). Its first discussion in October saw it postpone further discussion till 1926, on the assumption that the Royal Commission on the Coal industry, appointed in September 1925, would not report till then. The Industrial Committee's next meeting in December recommended that the General Council should not seek the additional powers urged at the TUC conference. Citrine raised the issue of preparations in January but consideration of this was postponed till a meeting could take place with the miners. This meeting, on 19 February, in turn agreed to leave the issue till the Royal Commission report had been published. Apart from a re-statement of support for the miners' position in February, nothing further was done. Ramsay MacDonald asked for a meeting on 3 March, just ahead of the publication of the report. The miners refused if Jimmy Thomas, the right-wing leader of the rail union, was to be present. On 8 March the Minister of Labour, Steel-Maitland, also asked for meetings. The report itself was published on 10 March and the government gave its response on 24 March – that there must be mutual agreement between the owners and miners – but by mid-April any attempt at such negotiations had broken down. The first discussion at General Council took place on 27 April within four days of the deadline when the subsidy would expire and the mine owners would seek to impose wage cuts to be negotiated separately at district level.

It is difficult to be entirely sure of intentions on the government side. The Tory right wing wanted a showdown with the trade union movement from the start. Baldwin's strategy is not so obvious. His public position

12 *Sunday Worker*, 22 November 1925; James Klugmann, *History of the Communist Party of Great Britain, Volume 2: The General Strike 1925–1926* (Lawrence and Wishart, 1969).

13 R. Taylor, 'Citrine's Unexpurgated Diaries 1925–26', *Historical Studies in Industrial Relations*, 2005, vol.20, no.1, pp.67–102.

was to seek agreement through negotiation, insisting that it was a matter for the two sides of the industry and not the government itself. The Royal Commission was intended to facilitate this. Yet he fully backed the detailed and meticulous preparations – involving all government departments and the army and navy – needed to defeat any attempt at a general strike, at the same time as insisting that the full scale of these preparation was not made public. His ally Steel-Maitland blocked any pre-strike call for volunteers and other public pronouncements.[14] For Baldwin the government had to be seen as a facilitator for industrial peace.

Yet there is no convincing evidence that Baldwin did not, more or less from the beginning, see a showdown with the unions, ending in their humiliating defeat, as a necessary part of his strategy for 're-educating' and constitutionalising Labour. After stigmatising and isolating the Communist Left, it still remained to demonstrate to those who thought like Bevin, and remained committed to political strike action, that such unconstitutional pressure on the government was not going to work.

Bevin, in his New Year message to members for 1926, had struck a confident note. He detailed the growing strength of the TGWU. Membership was sharply up. Financially the union had wiped out its deficit and now had a considerable reserve. Money was laid aside for the construction of the union's massive new headquarters in a prime spot close to parliament. 'We are, in fact, beginning to reap the advantages of unification'.[15] Organisationally he praised the democracy displayed by the union's second 1925 biennial conference as essential for the operation of a general union the size of the TGWU. Members could see, in the detailed voting, that they themselves made the key decisions. But he warned 'the great question looming for 1926 [...] is the Miners' and then castigates the mine owners: 'one can feel that their fellow capitalists must be feeling in a state of absolute despair at their complete incompetence'. The mine owners had implacably opposed industrial reorganisation and remained insistent that wages must come down, that national agreements end and that bargaining take place at regional and even pit level to reflect local costs in what remained a totally disorganised industry.

Defending the Miners: Defending the TGWU

As leader of the TGWU Bevin had two immediate concerns. One was that in any strike action it should not be the transport unions alone that bore the brunt of solidarity action – as would have been largely the case in July 1925. He was insistent that the number of participating unions be broadened. His

14   TNA CAB 24 175/62. Steel Maitland, 6 November 1925.
15   *The Record*, January 1926.

second concern, however, was that if the mine owners got their way and the coal industry forced back to district-level bargaining, this would set a wider precedent. If this principle were transferred to all industries, it would destroy the organisational base of the TGWU, which largely relied on national-level agreements in the docks and passenger transport and specialist industries such as flour milling, galvanising, chemicals and confectionary, to sustain its membership. Such national level agreements he saw as essential for the viability of any general union like the TGWU mainly organised among casualised workers without the protection of skilled qualifications.

Bevin also knew that in the event of a strike, even if the miners fought alone, the TGWU could not avoid involvement. As a union it organised a section of the coal workforce itself, coal trimmers and surface men loading coal. Additionally, many of the TGWU organised workers in docks and canals were largely dependent on coal transport. More politically, in terms of union cohesion, Bevin was aware that there would be strong rank-and-file calls for solidarity action to halt coal movements whatever position the leadership took. While the TUC had so far done little or nothing to develop local organisation, the Minority Movement – with the backing of a significant number of trades and labour councils – had already begun organising Councils of Action on the 1920 model. And on the ground, in terms of everyday trade union activity, Bevin would have been aware that members were demonstrating a significant level of assertiveness. Of the hundred or so major disputes listed in the *Ministry of Labour Gazette* over the 12 months up to May 1926, a full 10 per cent were over refusals to work with non-trade unionists.

Baldwin: 'Save Our Constitutional Government'

The six weeks following the publication of the Coal Commission report saw a flurry of behind-the-scenes activity by the government in which Bevin appears to have had considerable involvement. Steel-Maitland and Sir Horace Wilson, permanent secretary at the Ministry of Labour, held a series of discussions with him, drawing on Bevin's own consultations with A.J. Cook and others of the miners' leaders.

These pre-strike discussions may have been designed to assess the basis for an agreement. They may have been an attempt to identify differences and weaknesses among the trade union leaders as in 1921. Or possibly both. Baldwin remained adamant that it was for the miners and mine owners themselves to resolve the dispute between them. The government might later take action on some of the technical recommendations of the Royal Commission report. But the government could not impose a settlement. Nor would it continue to subsidise wages.

In the final three days of intense negotiation before the strike notices went out on 3 May, Bevin became the principal mediator between the

General Council and the miners, Ramsay MacDonald and the government, both in official negotiations and behind the scenes. Yet ultimately in the final negotiations on 2 and 3 May, the government appears to have lost interest in a settlement, even when the General Council offered a formula that could include a cut in wages. Famously the General Council, meeting separately at Downing Street till late at night, knocked on the prime minister's door to discuss terms. They were told he had gone away. Why?

It may have been, as Baldwin was keen to suggest later, that the right wing had gained ascendance in the Cabinet and that the printers' refusal to print the anti-union *Daily Mail* made it impossible to continue negotiations.[16] Or, no less likely, it may have been that Baldwin saw exactly the opportunity he wanted now that the notices for a general strike had been sent out. The union leaders had committed themselves and could not draw back. The issue was no longer that of miners' pay but the illegality of TUC tactics, i.e. using the collective strength of labour to bring pressure to bear on a constitutional government. Birkenhead and Churchill got the blame for the breakdown while Baldwin remained the man of peace. By delay and prevarication he had succeeded in switching the issue to the defence of the Constitution.

In Downing Street the day after negotiations collapsed, the deputy Cabinet Secretary Tom Jones noted down the prime minister's comments on Bevin's role in the negotiations: 'we agreed Bevin was the most powerful member of the TUC. The PM said that Steel-Maitland and Wilson had seen a lot of him and were well disposed to him but the PM himself was doubtful. Ramsay is a Kerenski and Kerenskis have lost control. Bevin may well picture himself as the Napoleon of the trade union movement'.[17]

Bevin maintained a hatred of Baldwin to the end of his days, describing him in 1929 as the 'most callous man who has ever sat in the House of Commons'.[18]

---

16 This action was taken spontaneously by the print workers themselves and was in no way official action by the main printing union NATSOPA: R. Suthers, *History of NATSOPA* (London, 1929) and as amplified in the 1964 edition by the editor J. Moran.
17 Alexander Kerensky was Chair of the Russian Provisional Government that lost power to the Bolsheviks in November 1917. K. Middlemas (ed.), *Thomas Jones: Whitehall Diaries*, vol.2 (Oxford University Press, 1969), p.38.
18 *The Record*, January 1929; E. Bevin 'Old Year and New'.

5

The General Strike 1926

In which the government is taught a lesson but then tricks the
TUC leaders

Despite the TUC's almost complete lack of central organisation, the response to the strike call far exceeded expectations. On the first day, only a section of the total workforce had been called out. This first wave was composed principally of transport workers: railways, docks, passenger transport and power workers as well as printing, iron and steel, metal, chemicals and building. Many were members of the TGWU. Engineering, textiles, shipbuilding, distributive trades, the post office and wood workers remained at work, until eventually receiving strike notices on 11 May. But the response from the first wave was virtually 100 per cent, with many non-unionists joining as well.

Near 100 per cent Solidarity

On the railways, using Bullock's figures, 0.014 per cent of train drivers turned up for work on the first day on the London, Midland and Scottish railways, 0.011 per cent of firemen and 0.015 per cent of guards. In London none of the LGOC's 3,293 buses moved.[1] Even in the second week, using volunteers and members of the territorial army, the transport companies were only able to operate token services. No more than a hundred trams ever ran in London; even fewer reached their destinations. The docks were totally silent until the navy ratings moved in and worked under cover of machine guns and armoured cars, again shifting only token amounts. And, as Bullock also points out, the decision to join the strike

---

1 Bullock, *Life & Times of Ernest Bevin*, I, pp.316–317.

was not an easy one. All those joining were legally breaking their contracts and thereby rendering themselves liable to loss of future employment and any occupational pensions to which they were entitled.[2]

Initially central organisation was almost entirely lacking. The TUC had made no preparations. Strike calls went out from individual unions. The assumption, up until the beginning of May, would seem to have been that some sort of temporary resolution would have been found on the basis of the Royal Commission report. Once the strike began the small TUC office staff was overwhelmed with demands for instructions and information – and with the General Council in constant session there was no effective guidance. At the end of the first day Bevin secured agreement for the creation of a small strike organising committee, chaired by the Left-winger Purcell, within which Bevin – much to Citrine's annoyance – was the dominant figure. Bevin immediately decentralised and established committees with specific functions as far as possible outside the TUC building: transport and food permits at the NUR headquarters, a building committee for regulating any permitted construction work at the Building Trade Workers' offices in Clapham. The regulation of public services was delegated to the employee representatives on the Joint Industrial Council for Electricity and Gas. Additionally, there were committees for intelligence, publicity (producing the daily *British Worker*), an interviewing committee for communications and receiving delegations and a propaganda committee to organise meetings and speakers. While Citrine resented Bevin's intervention as self-aggrandising and bumptious, the organisation worked. At local level, striking unions were asked to set up joint organising committees. Telegrams flowed back and forward. The code word for satisfactory operations was 'constitutional'.

'Refrain from Starting Work on 12 May'

At TGWU headquarters, Bevin had telegrammed out to all striking sections on 1 May. 350,000 TGWU members came out in the first wave. Local organisation, including the payment of strike pay, was left in the hands of area secretaries and, with powers delegated regionally, there is limited correspondence in the central files. Most were reports of 100 per cent compliance – like that from the Yorkshire area secretary on the third day of the strike. 'We are getting a better position day by day'. But, he added, keeping some sections working was confusing. 'I only hope that the time is not far distant when we get an order that all transport must stop'. Bevin sent out telegrams on the same day reporting that the number of men on strike has 'increased today both on transport

2 Ibid., p.316.

and amongst general workers' and the wireless report that Cardiff docks were working was 'completely false'. Three days later, 9 May, he reports the situation as 'excellent'. In Bath and Swindon 'such a response has never been known before'. In Plymouth the town clerk had agreed to end all arrangements with the government's Organisation for the Maintenance of Supply (OMS). In Belfast dockers 'will refuse to unload any steamer loaded by blacklegs'. The following day instructions went out that all transport permits to be cancelled. Every transport worker was to be on strike, with the only exception being Co-op milk deliveries. On 11 May instructions were issued for all engineering and shipbuilding workers to 'refrain from starting work' on Wednesday 12 May. And Bevin also noted the still-growing support for strike: 'in certain districts a display of force is being made but throughout the country the strikers are orderly and the situation solid. New groups of workers are coming out rather than work with imported labour or handle tainted goods. All our reports from every area show all sections are standing firm'. In a second telegram he added: 'Reports continue to show that large numbers non-unionists on strike everywhere are enrolling in their appropriate unions and joining in the strike and refusing to work with blacklegs. On the East Coast boilermakers and other skilled workers on the docks voluntarily stopped yesterday because of the introduction of the military'.[3]

Yet on the same day, 11 May, behind-the-scenes negotiations, largely led by J.H. Thomas, were taking place, also involving Bevin and Sir Herbert Samuel, previously chair of the Royal Commission.

The Government Finds Its Preparations Inadequate

The government was taken aback by the scale and effectiveness of the strike. It had expected the response to be partial and for the strike to begin disintegrating relatively quickly. It did not.

The government's biggest immediate concern was the effectiveness of the blockade on transport and docks and supplies of petrol and food. Its strategy had been mainly based on the Navy – moving troops quickly and invisibly, around the coasts, supplying ratings to work the docks and for its great battle cruisers to act as floating offshore power stations to replace those on land. But it was not prepared for the complete immobilisation of all transport. Nor had it bargained for the mass pickets that blocked its attempts to distribute supplies, particularly in the capital. Government convoys mainly had to pass from the Thames docks through the East End where the population and local councils were solidly against them. Existing

---

3 MRC MSS 126/TG/11/1/26 (Areas and branches to centre); TG/11/1/9 Centre to Areas and branches.

police forces were quite inadequate. By 6 May government petrol supplies were running low. Although troops and armoured cars guarded convoys, the government was frightened of precipitating a direct confrontation between soldiers and civilian crowds, and Citrine's diary contains reports that some of the regiments had been confined to barracks on account of fears as to their reliability.

On 7 May, the fourth day of the strike, the situation was judged so serious that the Cabinet decided to mobilise the Territorial Army (TA) and, because of their undoubted class loyalty, the Officer Training Corps (OTC) at the public schools and universities. It was stipulated, in order to stress the 'civilian' character of government support, that they be enrolled as special constables and equipped with batons. But, however complete the government's proclaimed preparations, the Home Office did not have anything like enough batons, a deficiency that had to be made good by a night-time convoy from Whitehall to High Wycombe to pick up 27,000 chair legs from the furniture manufacturers.[4] The embodiment of the OTC and the TA on 8 and 9 May resulted in what was described as police riots when the new 'special constables' were unleashed on pickets. Although this temporarily enabled some armoured convoys to reach their destination, it further heightened antagonism between working-class communities and the government. Over the same period there were widespread arrests of those involved with the Councils of Action, and particularly communists, and the seizure of equipment for producing leaflets and strike bulletins.

By this stage cabinet members appear to have been seriously worried about developments. One of the major figures among the coal owners, Lord Crawford, met the hard-line Lord Birkenhead and the Minister for Labour, Steel-Maitland, for informal talks on 10 May. He described them both as 'in a fright'.[5] Lord Birkenhead had in fact spent the first two days of the strike composing lengthy memoranda disputing claims that he personally had been responsible for the breakdown in negotiations. Friday 10 May also saw Lord Reith at the BBC take over the reading of (government-produced) news bulletins because of complaints that the regular announcers 'sounded panicky'.[6] Lord Robert Cecil, who left the country on 7 May, commented the strike could last weeks if the revolutionaries maintained their pressure on the TUC leaders.[7]

After the end of the strike, the Treasury conducted its own audit of how well the government machine had responded. Large sections of the

---

4   TNA MEPOL 5/135. 27,000 'truncheons' were secured in this way overnight on 7/8 May.

5   Quentin Outram, 'Class Warriors: The Coalowners', in J. McIlroy (ed.), *Industrial Politics and the Mining Lockout* (University of Wales Press, 2004) p.121.

6   C. Stuart (ed.), *The Reith Diaries* (Harper Collins, 1977), p.246.

7   TNA CAB 24 178/88. Cecil to Cabinet.

The General Strike in London

Danny Freeman

Figure 2: TGWU banner on a Camberwell Strike demonstration

Credit: Reproduced from Andrew Murray, *The T&G Story: A History of the Transport and General Workers Union 1922–2007* (London, Lawrence and Wishart, 2008), p.58

As a teenager, future TGWU member and dockers' leader, Jack Dash, witnessed the mass resistance in south London to attempts by the authorities to break the strike:

> It was a Sunday, early evening, and there had been a demonstration in every London borough. I was at Elephant and Castle in Southwark and caught up with the terrific excitement of the crowd. Suddenly everyone was shouting abuse. All eyes were turned in one direction. Coming in from the direction of Westminster were carloads of Special Reserves, all steel-helmeted, truncheons at the ready, the trucks protected with a kind of wire cage to protect them from the missiles thrown by strikers. They were followed by Mounted Police, escorting a General omnibus with passengers, driven by a university student. [...] Stones began to rain down from the tops of adjacent tenement buildings onto the armoured vehicles. The mounted reserves and police were unseated from their horses. Running fights took place

with the foot police. The bus was halted, the passengers dragged out, a great crowd of men overturned the bus, which caught fire and began to blaze away. (Jack Dash, *Good Morning, Brothers!* (Mayflower, 1970), p.18.)

This was on Sunday 9 May. Elephant and Castle was a strategic point. Southwark provided the base for one of London's biggest bus companies, Tillings, and was at the industrial heart of South London with docks, engineering and printing works. Six major roads came together at Elephant and Castle. Council of Action stewards, distinguished by red arm bands, tried to ensure that only traffic with permits from the TUC was allowed through. The previous day a scab bus driver had knocked down a motor cyclist and mounted the pavement, killing two people.

Jack Dash comments on the community-wide response to the strike call: 'everyone was involved and the solidarity was strong. The poverty in the area was great but the friendship was too – a question of bread and butter' (Ibid., p.17).

Throughout Southwark all trams had stopped at the outset. On Wednesday 5 May, after naval ratings had taken control of the power station, an attempt was made to restart the trams using volunteers. A large group of strikers and their wives had gathered outside the depot and even the very large number of police and OMS could not stop them from smashing the tram windows and pushing it back. At the Surrey docks only seven men out of 2,000 turned up for work on the first day. The TGWU reported 'wonderful solidarity' from the Port of London clerical and supervisory staff, their first ever strike. On Friday 7 May, as food supplies in London began to run short, the government tried to introduce 'volunteers'. Eighty were taken to the riverside. But 'the police protection was so long in arriving that when it had arrived the eighty men were found to be missing'. Later in the weekend naval ratings were brought in and some food taken up the Thames in barges (Django, 2011, 'Nine Days in May: the 1926 General Strike in Southwark', *libcom.org*, 10 July, https://libcom.org/history/nine-days-may-1926-general-strike-southwark).

Further east at Deptford the strike was totally solid. As in most boroughs across the East End, where there were Labour-controlled councils and a tradition of resistance to the government, the council gave official backing to the strike committee. All co-operation with government agencies ceased. The strike committee itself was jointly established by the Trades Council, the Labour Party and the local National Unemployed Workers Committee Movement. Politically it united all sections of the Left. Virtually all workplaces stopped, not just those in the 'first wave'. The London district of the Amalgamated Engineering Union (AEU) had called on its members to come out immediately and helped provide mass pickets everywhere. For the first time in its history the Royal Navy Victualling Yard came out along with Woolwich Arsenal. Workers at the non-union United Glass Company bottle works struck work, with 750 joining the TGWU. Even out in suburban Lewisham discipline seems to have been strong. All those in the 'first wave' came out, transport was halted and union officials had difficulty keeping the second wave at work. Building workers at the new LCC estate at Downham had to be repeatedly told to resume work (John Attfield and John Lee, 'Deptford and Lewisham', in J. Skelley (ed.), *The General Strike* (Lawrence and Wishart, 1976), pp.261–282).

Across the river the shutdown was almost total. Labour controlled the borough councils in Poplar, Stepney, Bethnal Green and West Ham. All had closed down their power stations. 'No blackleg driver dared go east of Aldgate' (Julie Jacobs, 'From Hackney', in Skelley, *General Strike*, pp.360–367).

Even in Hackney, where there was a combined Liberal–Conservative controlled council protected by a regular army detachment at Hackney Wick and a major encampment in nearby Victoria Park, the police remained on the defensive. On Wednesday 5 May the police surprised the small picket at the Mare Street tram depot and escorted a large number of volunteers inside with the intention of operating a tram service. Within an hour the depot was totally surrounded. By evening the police superintendent was pleading with the Council of Action to release the imprisoned volunteers. Here also 'second line' factories were closed early on in the strike: Bergers Paint at Hackney Wick, Polikoff Clothes in Well Street and Zinkins Furniture in Mare Street (Ibid.).

government's preparations, it concluded, had been well designed and operated effectively. This was particularly so for the use of the Navy to deploy troops, distribute supplies and provide emergency energy. Also very effective had been the control of news, especially through the BBC, and communications with regional controllers. Where the report expressed great concern was over the degree to which the town councils responsible for local services had ceded authority to strike committees. There had been widespread negotiations over supplies. Transport permits issued by strike committees had assumed official status while government notices had been removed. In one case even the military command had had to negotiate with a local Council of Action to secure the supply of food to feed troops. In the future, it argued, this had to be avoided at all costs. It led directly to the progressive breakdown of state authority and a situation of dual power.[8]

8 TNA T 163/26 file 62020/011.

From the Autobiography of Frederick Cotton, London Member of the National Union of Vehicle Builders

Figure 3: Frederick Cotton

Credit: Photo courtesy of Frederick Cotton's great-niece

Frederick Cotton was 24 at the time of the strike. A member of the National Union of Vehicle Builders, he worked at trimming and finishing luxury cars in London's West End. Yet, despite vehicle builders not being officially called out in the first wave and the 'luxury' character of the product, the entire workplace seems to have come out on strike immediately in the first wave.

The following year, 1925, I got a job at Hoopers in Kings Road, Chelsea. I worked under the foreman trimmer, Jimmy Woodlands. I have never been so unhappy in a job; this foreman stands out in my mind as a tyrant. He had taught coach trimming at London Polytechnic. I could not do anything right for him; he sapped my confidence. Like a lot of the leading coach builders of those days, there was always a clique of cronies of the foreman. This led to a lot of abuses, blue-eyed boys who could do no wrong, and others who could do no right. So although I was desperate for a job, it was with a sense of relief that after the motor show, I was sacked. My son Freddie was then about a year old. I wrote to Barkers Coach Builders of Olaf Street, North Kensington, a stone's throw from the place where I first saw light of day. It was to be one of those strokes of luck. Barkers & Co. were established in the eighteenth century. They now built bodies for Rolls Royce' chassis mostly, with occasionally Italian Isotta Fraschini, Hispano-Suiza and Belgian Minerva. They had records of work done for the Duke of Wellington of Waterloo fame. However, it was not until February 1926 that I had an answer to my letter, inviting me to go for interview. The upshot was that I got the job, helped by the fact that I had worked for some of the other leading coach builders. I started there on 3 March 1926 for what was to prove a considerable run of five years, some of the happiest working days of my life. After doing nothing right for the foreman at Hoopers, here at Barkers, I seemed successful from the beginning. Syd Wareham was a totally different man to work under from the beginning, he seemed to bring out the best in his men. He would always listen, and would defend them if he thought they were right, against the higher management. The work here was first class. There were two grades of pay, 1s 11d an hour for top men, 1s 9d for the lower grade, of which I was one. Some of the finest craftsmen in the trade were there. They had a sports club to which nearly all of the employees paid a little each week, and a sports ground at East Acton, another attraction for me. I joined the football section at once, and played for the team. Of course, it was the year of the General Strike, which started at the end of April. I was a member of the National Union of Vehicle Builders, which came out immediately; the whole of the factory was closed down and the pickets put on. My daughter Thelma was born on 24 April.

For the period we were out, things seemed to be against me; my sympathies were with the miners, naturally; the strike was almost complete, with the working people of the country solidly behind them; so much so that the trade union leaders like Thomas, Citrine and others either got cold feet or were traitors. Through the TUC they instructed the men on strike to return to work, without a negotiated agreement of conditions of that return. The men were astounded; some were victimised and sacked in unorganised shops. Barkers was an organised shop, nearly 100 per cent trade unionists. Even here, some of the directors wanted to sack all men over 30 years of age until it was pointed out to them that these men were some of the finest craftsmen in the trade and irreplaceable. So the miners were left to battle on with the mine owners of those days, for six months, until they were starved into submission. In fact, the miners were locked out until they accepted a reduction in pay (incidentally, their third reduction in pay since World War One). The politicians of the day insisting that the Germans pay reparations to the victors, and with Germany being almost bankrupt and unable to pay in currency, it was decided that they could pay in goods, among their coal. So, there we were, sitting on an island of coal, with German coal dumped on our doorstep. The Welsh miners, who dug and tunnelled to blow up Hill 60 in the war, heroes then, were victims of the reparations in the aftermath of the war.

With the return of the vehicle builders to the various places of work, I resumed my job with Barkers. One could say that without exception, their customers were millionaires.

The National Union of Vehicle Builders amalgamated with the TGWU in 1973.

Scotland's Transport Workers and Dockers

Robert Laurie, Allan Marshall, Vince Mills
and Hugh Maguiness

Figure 4: A bus which failed to reach Glasgow

Credit: © Herald and Time Group. Reproduced by kind permission of
the Herald Times Picture Library

A joint organisation committee of all participating Scottish unions was formed by the Scottish Trades Union Congress (STUC) on 3 May. The same day, a meeting of all Scottish passenger transport unions took place in the TGWU offices in Glasgow including the NUR, ASLEF, Railway Clerks and the National Union of Seamen (NUS). In the evening there were mass meetings of tramway workers in the Berkeley Halls in Glasgow and of commercial transport drivers in the Central Halls (*Evening Times,* 3 May).

The strike appears to have been complete across Scotland. Minimal train and bus services were run by scabs – but they were neither reliable nor safe (three people died in a train crash in Edinburgh) ('Paisley Strike Bulletin', 11 May, as reproduced in Iain MacDougall, 'General Strike Bulletins', *Miscellany of the Scottish History Society,* vol.12 (Pillans & Wilson Ltd., 1994), pp.170ff).

In Glasgow it took a day or two for the authorities to put together a minimal bus service based on volunteer strike-breakers. Glasgow city council, then under Conservative control, together with its fiercely anti-union tramway manager Colonel Dalrymple, sought to mobilise university students, volunteer strike-breakers and special constables and a very small minority of non-union workers who had refused to join the union.

On 4 May the first scab buses were attacked and overturned as they ran down the Old Edinburgh Road to Parkhead (*Emergency Press*, 5 May; the *Emergency Press* was produced by a consortium of Glasgow newspapers led by the *Glasgow Herald*). By 5 May the authorities had been able to station a significant number of student scabs in the Ruby Street tram depot in the East End. The following morning at 4 a.m., five hundred miners marched in from Cambuslang to assist the TGWU pickets. As the police battled to shift the pickets, rioting spread through the east end of the city. Mounted police and 'specials' attacked with batons and considerable injuries were inflicted, one critical, and 60 arrests made. Strikers and their supporters regrouped and further conflict occurred that evening with crowds blocking streets at Bell Street and Great Hamilton Street and two strikers hospitalised after repeated baton changes by mounted police (*Emergency Press*, 6 May). The following evening 'dense crowds' gathered in central Glasgow. Renfrew, Renfield and Sauchiehall Streets were 'completely blocked' to halt traffic. Again mounted and foot police were deployed. The crowds were 'dispersed only to gather again in different areas' (*Emergency Press*, 7 and 8 May).

The following day, 8 May, a determined effort was made to halt trams from the Springburn depot in Glasgow. According to subsequent police court proceedings, 'a large and disorderly crowd' led by Councillor Alexander Mathieson waylaid a tram staffed by a tram worker who had refused to join the union. According to the subsequent police court report, 'so serious was the situation in Springburn that no other cars were run from that depot' (*Evening Times*, 26 May).

In Edinburgh similar battles took place as the authorities sought to assert control in Scotland's capital. On 6 May pitch battles took place on the high street with baton charges by mounted and foot police. There were a number of injuries including four police, one critical (*Emergency Press*, 7 May). Outside Scotland's two capital cities, efforts to run services were much more spasmodic. Lanark announced the suspension of all services on 6 May (*Emergency Press*, 7 May). In mining areas, which included much of Lanarkshire, Ayrshire, the Lothians and Fife, the authorities kept a very low profile and the strikers tended to take the fight to the police. In Tranent on 7 May, after the police had attacked pickets, the police station was stormed (*Emergency Press*, 8 May). In Kilmarnock no services ran. Nor did they run in the Vale of Leven. Many strike committees posted pickets on roads to halt transport. Bathgate patrolled the Glasgow–Edinburgh road. In Fife a number of local strike committees maintained motorcycle corps for this purpose. East Wemyss, Lochgelly and Bowhill did so (Edinburgh and District *Strike Bulletin*, 9 May). Methil Council of Action had 150 motorcycles and a 750-strong workers' defence corps. On 6 May it took over Buckhaven council and re-appointed its officials to implement strike committee policy for social welfare and other social services (Methil *Strike Bulletin*, 5, 6 and 7 May).

In the docks, on the Clyde, at Leith, Grangemouth, Dundee and Aberdeen nothing moved for the first days of the strike. The battleship *Comus* had moved up the Clyde on 4 May joined by a flotilla of smaller warships (*Emergency Press*, 4 May). On 10 May naval ratings were ordered ashore at Glasgow docks and provided an armed guard for strike-breakers, described as 'unused to manual labour', unloading food supplies from 'a number of vessels' (*Evening Times*, 1 June). This seems to have been the only attempt by the authorities to regain control of the docks. On 15 May the *Evening Times* reports two transatlantic liners as sailing from Glasgow with no cargo. There appears to have been no settlement acceptable to the dockers till 20 May (*Evening Times*, 21 May). In general commercial road transport seems also to have been effectively halted. A permit system was operated by local strike committees for essential supplies such as milk and bread.

Was there weakening towards the end? In Glasgow the authorities claimed to have reopened the subway 'with a modified service' and one suburban rail-line – although the Ladybank Joint Strike Committee bulletin for 11 May reports that only 28 train journeys took place on the West of Scotland rail network out of a previous daily total of 14,000. In general, strike organisation was improving and workers in the second wave were demanding to come out before 10 May. Some, such as the Albion works, Barclay Engineering and Kilmarnock Engineering did come out early (Partick *Strike Bulletin*, 9 and 10 May).

In terms of organisation the Left seemed to be dominant in Glasgow. It had secured majority control of the trades council strike committee at the outset and on 5 May won the vote to establish organising committees in the city's working-class neighbourhoods. Over the following days local committees involving elected members of the city and parish councils, co-op organisers, and representatives of trade unions and tenants associations were set up in the main working-class areas, 11 in all. Local neighbourhoods increasingly fell under their control. As in the previous general strike of 1919, women were particularly active in picketing and stopping profiteering by small shopkeepers (Partick Strike Committee *Bulletin*, 12 May).

East and West Midlands

Graham Stevenson

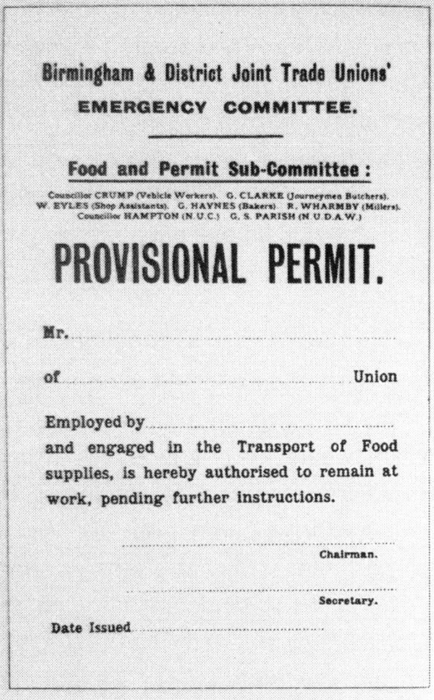

Birmingham & District Joint Trade Unions'
EMERGENCY COMMITTEE.

Food and Permit Sub-Committee :

Councillor CRUMP (Vehicle Workers).   G. CLARKE (Journeymen Butchers).
W. EYLES (Shop Assistants).   G. HAYNES (Bakers).   R. WHARMBY (Millers).
Councillor HAMPTON (N.U.C.)   G. S. PARISH (N.U.D.A.W.)

PROVISIONAL PERMIT.

Mr.

of .... Union

Employed by ....
and engaged in the Transport of Food
supplies, is hereby authorised to remain at
work, pending further instructions.

....
                                      Chairman.

....
                                      Secretary.

Date Issued ....

Figure 5: Birmingham official
strike permit

Credit: Birmingham Public Library,
'The Nine Days in Birmingham',
Birmingham Public Libraries Social
Sciences Department in associa-
tion with the WEA West Midlands
District 1976

TGWU membership in the East Midlands was largely restricted to bus and tram workers in its Passenger Services group – with some lorry drivers and carters in the Commercial Services group. But all seem to have struck solidly when called out.

All Trent Motor Traction bus services, the dominant company across East Midlands, stopped at midnight on 3 May and did not resume. Tram workers in Derby, Nottingham and Leicester also struck work from the first day. In Derby, where transport services were described as 'paralysed', the TGWU paid out strike pay at the Temperance Hall. A transport subcommittee was formed of road and rail unions with the title of Derby and District Joint Transport Strike Committee, with 21 delegates. As elsewhere it was given delegated authority by the TUC to deal with transport permits. In Leicester there were still no trams running on 10 May. Ripley, Mansfield, Northampton and Kettering reported no signs of weakening. United strike committees were set up and bulletins issued everywhere. Only the tiny Blue Bus Company of Willington kept going through the strike, albeit with only a minimal non-unionised service.

In the West Midlands, TGWU members were mainly organised in trams, buses, canals, a few in road haulage and as coal trimmers in the mining industry in the Black Country. Canals were important for industrial transport, especially for moving coal and coke, and the 1,000 bargees struck solidly – no doubt remembering the wider solidarity of the TGWU's support for their own strike in 1923. The main component of TGWU membership came from the old 'blue button' tram and bus workers union, the Amalgamated Tramway and Vehicle Workers (AATVW): its somewhat right-wing local secretary, Councillor Jim Crump, became the first TGWU secretary for Area 5. The AATVW brought 9,000 members including bus and taxi drivers, chauffeurs, carters and farriers across the West Midlands. Additionally, joining the TGWU in 1926 was the National Association of Enginemen, Firemen, Mechanics, Motormen and Electrical Workers – becoming the union's power group and particularly strong in Staffordshire.

In Birmingham, John Corrin, officer for the TGWU's commercial transport branch, became chair of the All-Union Birmingham Strike Committee. The committee's 21 members included representatives of virtually all unions in the Birmingham area. Despite the political weakness of Labour in Birmingham (there were no Labour MPs in 1926 and the council was dominated by the Conservatives) no buses or trams ran in Birmingham until 10 May when an attempt was made to restart services. On 5 May the strike committee reported to TUC headquarters: 'the extent of the stoppage is much greater than anyone anticipated and all road, passenger and carrying traffic has been stopped [...] on the railway the stoppage in complete [...] in the factories the difficulty is now to keep the people at work. All are anxious to be out and in the fight. Newspapers have failed to appear' (R. Hastings, 'The General Strike in Birmingham' in Skelley, *The General Strike*, pp.208–231, citing TUC Records HD 5366). Withdrawal of labour by electricians and engineers halted many of the big factories including Austin's Longbridge plant, Wolseley, the Birmingham Wagon Co. and the Metropolitan Wagon Works. Transport permits issued by the strike committee became more or less universal – causing the chief constable to issue an order declaring them to be illegal on 9 May (*Birmingham Post*, 10 May, cited in Hastings, 'General Strike').

Some weakening of the strike in transport appears to have taken place in the final days when the municipal tram undertaking issued a demand for the return of uniforms on 10 May. The same day the entire strike committee was arrested for reprinting a statement from the *Cricklewood Workers Gazette* that the government had been defeated in the Commons. Attempts were then made on 10 May to halt electricity supplies but had not been implemented at the time when the strike itself was halted by the TUC General Council.

In Wolverhampton and the Black Country the strike appears to have remained solid until the very end. In Wolverhampton, according to the pro-employer *Express and Star*, the bus company had to employ scab volunteers when it finally made an attempt to get some buses back on the road on 10 May. Upwards of 1,000 strikers assembled to halt their progress. A strike emergency committee had been convened at the beginning of the strike representing all unions, including the TGWU. Transport was completely halted. Strong pressure came from the engineers in the major factories to come out ahead of the 'second wave' and a majority appear to have ceased work (George Barnsby, 'The General Strike in the Black Country', in Skelley, *General Strike*, pp.193–208).

Yorkshire and Humberside

Mark Metcalf

Figure 6: Bradford Trades Council Strike Committee

Credit: From Mary Ashraf, *100 Years of Bradford Trades Council 1872–1972* (Bradford Trades Council, 1972). Reproduced by kind permission of Bradford Trades Council

The TGWU Yorkshire area secretary based in Leeds telegrammed the union's London headquarters on Thursday 6 May: 'We are getting a better position day by day'. But he added that keeping some sections at work was 'confusing'. 'I only hope that the time is not far distant when we shall get an order that all transport must stop' (MRC TG/11/1/26). Five days later, on Monday 10 May, the Leeds Trades and Labour Council central strike committee reported that rails were 100 per cent out and road transport 98 per cent out. Despatch riders were maintaining contact with Sheffield, Doncaster, Halifax, Huddersfield, York and Hill. All remained solid (T. Woodhouse, 'The General Strike in Leeds', *Northern History*, 1982, vol. 18, no. 1, 252–262).

In Halifax, up in the Pennines to the West, it was reported on Saturday 8 May that all rail services had ceased, strong pickets were on duty and even the station clock had stopped. All transport workers were on strike and there had been a full response in all other unions where workers had been called out including printers, wire workers, joiners and plumbers. All members of the Workers' Union were also out. On Saturday 8 May 10,000 attended a mass rally in Savile Park, the 'largest in many years'. The local paper, *The Courier*, reported that during the following week 'more operatives were brought out on strike'. The scale of the response in Halifax, as elsewhere in West Yorkshire, may have been related to the victory secured by the 150,000 woollen and worsted workers in their three-week strike the previous summer, at the same time as Red Friday.

Bradford to the south was highlighted as an example of effective strike organisation. Laybourn reports a Council of Action being formed on Monday 3 May – motion moved by the president and secretary of the Trades Council. A subcommittee was established on the Tuesday to deal with transport permits and separate committees to deal with transport, engineering, textiles and miscellaneous (K. Laybourn, *The General Strike of 1926*, Manchester 1993). Not a single train ran after 3 May. When on Tuesday 11 May an attempt was made to introduce a skeleton tram service, the Engineering Group gave instructions for the withdrawal of all powerhouse men from power station in Valley Road. This ended the tram service ('Barbour to Citrine, 21 May 1926', West Yorkshire District Archive Item 57 and 57/1). Bradford Council of Action issued its own printed bulletin, the *Bradford Worker*, totalling 26,500 copies by the end of strike, despite contrary instructions from TUC headquarters. The Council of Action at Morley a bit further to the south reported on Tuesday 11 May 'firmness and determination maintained at a meeting just held'. The following day, Wednesday 12, Keighley to the north reported that 'the situation here is as good as ever'. There is no evidence of any weakening of the strike.

Reading: TGWU South East Region

by Keith Jerrome (UNITE Community Branch)

On Sunday 2 May 1926 the Annual Labour Parade took place in Reading. The speeches and celebration went unreported since the following day was the first meeting of the Central Strike Emergency Committee (J. Goodwin 'The General Strike in Reading', M.Sc. Econ. Hist. London School of Economics in Local History Collection, Reading Central Library). The General Strike had commenced.

Two groups of unions maintained separate strike committees: the Joint Transport Group of TGWU, NUR, ASLEF and the Printing Group strike committee of the Typographical Association, the Lithographers and Papermakers etc. These two groups sent delegates to the Central Strike Emergency Committee which was composed of representatives from transport, building, printing and paper and metalworkers together with the chairman and secretary of the Trades Council. The centre of operations and the public focus for the strike was the Reading Trades Union Club in Minster Street (Borough Record Office ref. D/EX1216). It was the source for news with crowds awaiting the daily bulletins. A letter was sent to the strike committee by Arthur Pugh, the president and Walter Citrine, the acting secretary of the General Council of the TUC requiring the establishment of a communications machinery, a task which fell to the Dispatch and Transport Subcommittee of the Central Strike Committee (CSEC). The letter stated: 'The Driver will call on his return for information on the general position in the places your Committee have had placed under your jurisdiction'.

For Route 5 London–Plymouth on 6–7 May, the position for Reading was: 'Great activity at Labour Hd'quarters, Not a Tram, Few Buses, Pickets everywhere, Streets full of strikers, response has been magnificent, The Headquarters seems as big, well organised as Ecclestone Square,(London HQ TUC) Splendid series of Riders for communications'. Not only did the TUC provide routes for dispatch riders, on 6 May they added: 'Messengers should wire immediately from each town and after reaching their objective'. A telegram of the same day states 'Reading absolute provided, Lansbury' which decoded meant: 'Reading, arrangements working well, spirit good'.

Arthur Lockwood, Secretary of Reading General Strike Emergency Committee sent progress reports on 5 and 6 May:

5 May Dear Sir
The position in Reading is very satisfactory. Railwaymen absolutely solid. All building stopped, except on Housing Schemes. Transport Workers solid. Six Corporation buses put on the street this afternoon, applying special 2d. Fares.

Meetings and Football Matches every day. A silver cup has been given for competition.

Biscuit Factory still at work. Packing Department likely to close down shortly owing to no empties.

Brewery Workers will cease work tomorrow night. The spirit of all is excellent.

6 May Dear Comrade

I have to report the only breach that has been made in the solid front is that the Corporation have been able to put six motor buses on the road. These are being handled by Inspectors and one or two by O.M.S. [Organisation for the Maintenance of Supplies].

Vehicle Builders have been withdrawn from Corporation Depot and other places. A few Biscuit Workers are now out in consequence of shortage of tins and Brewery Workers will be withdrawn tonight. Ranks absolutely solid, spirit magnificent.

Yours fraternally

The Transport Workers' Joint Strike Committee report of 6 May, written using the headed notepaper of the National Union of Railwaymen, indicated: 'Rail position solid [...] All Brewery Workers finish today [...] RCA (Railway Clerks Association) URS (United Road Services) and Road Transport Branches all working together for Victory'.

Arthur Lockwood had established the *Reading Citizen* and in 1924 Phoebe and Albert Cusden had assumed responsibility for it. In May 1926 it was published as a strike bulletin reproducing the national statements by the TUC General Council and union statements. Lockwood's letter of 6 May as secretary of CSEC was sent on the headed notepaper of Reading Trades Council and Labour Party. This had been established when the Trades Council acted to form Reading Labour Party in April 1918. On 6 May the former dockers' leader, president of the TGWU and chair of the TUC, Ben Tillett, addressed crowds in both the abbey ruins and Palmer Hall.

The Council's Tramways Committee, having a skeleton service run by 'loyal help of a few employees', issued the following notice on 7 May:

All men who have refused to carry out their duties since 3rd May must present themselves for duty not later than 7am on Saturday 8th May. Men who show their loyalty will receive the utmost support from the Tramways Committee after the strike under the Government measures. No man who does his duty loyally to the country in the present crisis will be left unprotected by the State from subsequent reprisals.

(County Borough of Reading, Public Notice to the Inhabitants of Reading, 7 May 1926)

The strike committee responded: 'The whole force and resources of the Trade Union Movement will be exerted in the interests of any man who may be refused reinstatement for taking a line of action that conscience and sense of justice dictated' (Goodwin, p.65). 'Tramways ultimatum expires at 7am. Skeleton tramway service restarts with police escort' (Goodwin, p.66).

Archibald Arding, Branch Secretary of the Vehicle Builders (NUVB), visited the Tramways depot on behalf of the branch committee to remonstrate with a member who had returned to work. Arding was accused of unlawfully intimidating a Mr and Mrs Deas and subsequently served one-month's hard labour. On his release on 11 June he was the guest at a large gathering of the Labour movement.

One hundred carpenters returned to work at the Railway Signal Works on 10 May and the following day TGWU and General and Municipal Workers Union (GMWU) members returned to work at Simonds Brewery while a call from the strike committee to the TUC sought a speaker with a national reputation to counteract wavering on the Tramways. The report from rider Mr W. Kenny for Route 10 London to Newbury stated: 'At Reading police raided offices on the 11th evening. Certain tramway men have been sacked. There was a big meeting held on the question. Missed Slough on return journey as wet through' (TUC Library General Strike collection: document in possession of author).

The same day, 11 May, moves were made to call out workers in Reading's big factories (biscuits and tin boxes) as part of the second wave. Ben Russell, secretary of the GMWU wrote on 11 May calling out members at Huntley and Palmers, at Serpells and at Huntley, Boorne & Stevens from Wednesday evening (Records of the GMB 1911–1988 Borough Record Office DEX2017). On Wednesday 12 May at 11 a.m. in the south breakfast room at the Huntley and Palmer factory, the firm's director Eric Palmer addressed the members of the firm's (non-union) workers' representation committee, revealing both the style of paternalist management and a relationship between union leaderships and big firms that excluded local members. He began by reading a letter from the Reading strike emergency committee which concluded 'Reading CSEC have decided to withdraw all labour from your establishment at the usual time of closing on Wednesday May 12th'. Mr Palmer continued:

> I am speaking with all the strength of my Board of Directors behind me. We had only dealt with National Officers of the union in the past, indeed no local official had ever been admitted to the Factory, the WRC [Workers Representation Committee] were elected by staff in the departments not in a Trade Union capacity though many if not all were members.

Mr Palmer did not recognise Arthur Lockwood and the RSEC. 'I cannot too strongly ask you to think, and think again, before you go and do such a mad rash thing – I cannot call it anything else – than to walk out of this place.' (Report of the Meeting of the WRC, 12 May 1926 under H&P 89, in the collection held by Reading University at the Museum of English Ruling Life).

In the chronology produced by Goodwin '1pm news filters through that General Strike has been called off'. The implication must be that as Mr Palmer was addressing 'our workpeople', the TUC General Council was meeting at Ecclestone Square and determining to end the General Strike. So we do not know how many H&P workers would have responded to the call of Ben Russell. Following the news, on the afternoon of Wednesday 12 May, a 'victory' procession headed for Caversham Bridge which was to have been opened by the Prince of Wales. That visit had been postponed, but the workers obliged by naming it 'Freedom Bridge'. The Trades Council and Labour Party held an interdenominational thanksgiving service at the London Street Primitive Methodist Church on 16 May.

By February 1927, 30 railwaymen still awaited reinstatement while GMWU members at Bradbeers Tin Works and Messers Timber Yard reported wage cuts. Archibald Arding of the NUVB was unemployed for five months following his release from prison and others who were unable to find work were rejected for aid by the board of guardians.

The Labour group on Reading borough council consisted of ten councillors. The Tories and Liberals combined to revise the committee structure reducing the size of key committees and then used their majority to exclude Labour members from six places. Alderman John Rabson, a councillor for 21 years, was due to take the first Labour mayorship and his was the only name before the selection committee, but the full council found an alternative choice. The Labour Party called a public meeting which considered and passed the resolution: 'That the attitude of the Borough Council concerning the Mayorality for 1927 is a travesty of impartiality and an insult to Trade Unionists and the poorer class of ratepayers' (Goodwin, pp.58–59).

The *Reading Citizen* of 15 January 1927 published the accounts for the Local General Strike Distress and Miners' Relief Fund. £1,191 9s 9d had been raised from trade unions, ward and women's sections plus house-to-house collections, donations and collection sheets. The Local Distress Fund received £309 19s 7d, the Women's Committee Fund got £762 7s 10d and over £100 went to miners and their families including the maintenance of miners' children in Reading. The miners fought on for six months experiencing terrible deprivation. They received assistance from workers worldwide.

The TUC General Council Walk into a Trap

From about 9 May, the NUR secretary and Labour leader J.H. Thomas (who, according to the Cabinet office, had applied for, and been given, police protection at the beginning of the strike) initiated detailed informal discussions with Sir Herbert Samuel, previously chair of the Royal Commission, who had come back from Italy.[9] Bevin quickly became involved as intermediary with the miners. Inconclusive discussions continued for two days using a draft Memorandum originally written by Samuel which appeared to concede the principle of government involvement if the miners agreed to the possibility of wage reductions in some districts. By 11 May it became clear that the miners would not accept any formulation that included a reduction in wages. Despite this Thomas, and Arthur Pugh as TUC president, persuaded the General Council to respond to this proposal for what was presumed to be a compromise settlement. On the evening of 11 May Baldwin phoned Bevin to see if the General Council wished to send a delegation. The invitation was postponed for a final attempt to persuade the miners and to avoid an open split. This failed. The General Council then agreed to proceed on the basis of the memorandum and for unions to suspend the strike notices. Notices were sent out for a return to work.

The following day the General Council delegation led by Thomas, Pugh and Bevin went to Downing Street. They were met outside the Cabinet office door by Sir Horace Wilson, permanent secretary at the Ministry of Labour, who asked for what reason they wanted to see the prime minister. According to Bevin's report, they replied 'we want to see him on the position'. Wilson replied: 'You know the prime minister will not see you until the strike is called off'. Thomas replied: 'we have come to call the strike off'.[10]

They were then ushered in to face Baldwin and six cabinet ministers. The government side included senior civil servants and stenographers taking verbatim notes (to be passed immediately to Reith at the BBC). They waited for Pugh and Thomas to open. In doing so, they made no mention of the Samuel memorandum or its stipulation that the mine owners withdraw their lockout notices. Nor was anything said about any guarantee to strikers of reinstatement. Baldwin's reply was brief – simply indicating the government's acknowledgement of their agreement to end the strike. It then dawned on the rest of the delegation that there was no agreement. The memorandum had no status. By agreeing that they had come to call off the strike and no more, they had walked into a trap.

9 Middlemass, *Thomas Jones: Whitehall Diaries*, Vol II, p.53.
10 MRC MSS 126/TG/11/1/24. Bevin's statement prepared for the 27 May meeting of area secretaries.

Ministers waited for Bevin to speak. Thomas and Pugh had said little about immediate circumstances. Bevin eventually came in, as he realised the enormity of the situation and the political challenges he would now face. He had to get his membership back to work. He had to end solidarity with the miners without securing any concession at all. He had do so in conditions where local employers were very likely to take the opportunity to penalise his own members. After facing down the Left just three years before, he was now exposed as never before to outrage from the rank and file. He could expect all his old enemies, no doubt led by Lansbury, to seek revenge.

He began 'we have taken a great risk in calling the strike off. I want to ask you if you could tell us whether you are prepared to make a general request as head of government for facilities for reinstatement to be given forthwith'. Baldwin declined to make any immediate commitment. Bevin continued to plead for some government commitment. Baldwin ended the meeting without giving any clear answer.[11]

Trickery had won the day. It is clear from his subsequent comments that Bevin believed that Thomas had deliberately led them to understand that the Samuel memorandum had government sanction. It did not. The government, however, was clearly aware of how the memorandum was being used and was being briefed at each stage. The following morning the government's *British Gazette* proclaimed 'Complete Surrender'.

Those returning to work found that employers were refusing employment to trade union activists and in some cases demanding wage reductions. In many workplaces it seems that workers spontaneously refused to commence. Bevin immediately telegrammed all areas that workers should come out on strike again and stay out. By the end of the day there were more workers out on strike than at any time over the previous nine days. It was at this point, with the country again totally immobilised, that Baldwin entered the Commons, according to Lansbury 'white as a ghost' (he was as frightened of his own backbenchers as he was of strikers), and made his Commons statement urging employers to take back all former strikers on the old conditions.[12]

11 TNA CAB 24 179/95.
12 *Lansbury's Labour Weekly*, 22 May 1926.

6

Co-operation and Incorporation
1926–27

*In which the Conservatives seek to assert ideological control over the
Labour movement*

The Government Re-considers its Strategy
and Changes Direction

In May 1926 Baldwin succeeded in outmanoeuvring the TUC leadership.
But in doing so he knew he had taken grave risks. He had dangerously
undermined the political credibility of the trade union and Labour Party
right-wingers on whom the government relied. And he had done so at
a time when the Left had, as never before, demonstrated the power of
direct working-class organisation in towns and cities across the country.
Although Ramsay MacDonald and Thomas redoubled their calls for the
Labour movement to abandon industrial action as a political tool, they
were met by renewed and, in the circumstances, very credible accusations
of treachery from *Lansbury's Labour Weekly* and the Minority Movement's
Sunday Worker.

The government quickly realised it had gravely underestimated the
potential strength of the British Labour movement and its support across
the country. Writing as he left the country on 7 May, Cecil had concluded
his memorandum to the Cabinet: 'the government must recognise it has
failed to overcome the distrust of working class, that at the next election
the electorate may vote for socialist measures and that as soon as strike is
conclusively won, government needs to compromise on social issues, such
as profit sharing, while at the same time making further general strikes
illegal'.[1]

---

1 TNA CAB 24 178/88. Robert Cecil, 7 May.

Five days after the end of the strike his brother, fellow cabinet member Lord Salisbury, went further. A year before he had been one of the most forthright in condemning the government surrender on Red Friday. Now he urged a major reversal of policy.

In a paper entitled 'Education: Trades Disputes Act and Partnership', he wrote of the 'urgent necessity of new policy' in the face of 'periodic crises of increasing intensity'. He was now convinced that 'the root of the matter is in the status of the worker' and that there is 'no hope that the present system can continue':

> Suspicion is not only widespread but has gradually grown in power and now developed into a settled conviction to have a change and since the war has assumed an urgent and dangerous character. Up to that date the workers sought their end in parliament [...]. The favourite method is now direct action, which is in its logical development revolution. Unless the government and parliament bestir themselves this change of method may become stereotyped, revolution may become a conviction. The worst of it is that unconstitutional pressure and direct action has been proved to be effective and the present triumph of the forces of order is an exception. If we look at the attitude of the workers and at their intentions – no doubt largely subconscious but no less formidable for that reason – the situation is essentially unstable. The worker is no longer content to be merely a hired machine of somebody else to do somebody else's work. He will be told, and he will partly believe it, that if the means of production are nationalised the work will be the nation's work and, as he is part of the nation, his own work.[2]

Salisbury's diagnosis (and language) is very similar to that of the Third [Communist] International (whose communiques he would have read weekly in the cabinet papers). But his proposals were somewhat different. He called on the government to work for a change in the structure of industry to incorporate workers and their unions into ownership through some form of share distribution and profit sharing. Co-operation should take place with business at the level of the firm. Significantly Salisbury's memorandum was headed 'Education'. These proposals were not unlike those advocated by Sir Alfred Mond, head of the giant Imperial Chemical Industries, although Mond placed more emphasis on co-operation at top level between national business management and union leaders.

For the government, in terms of negative assessments, worse was yet to come. Just after Salisbury wrote his memorandum, Labour won the

2 TNA CAB 24 179/95. Salisbury, 18 May 1926.

Hammersmith West by-election.[3] It was a constituency mainly populated by white-collar and middle-class voters and had previously been comfortably held by the Conservatives. Five days after the general strike, and in an election fought on the issue, there had been a 15 per cent swing to Labour, giving the party an absolute majority: 54 per cent of the vote over Liberals and Conservatives combined. The message was clear. It was the trade union movement and not the government that had won the propaganda war. A general election would see Labour in government with an absolute majority, whether led by a Kerensky or not.

The Cabinet hardliners, Churchill and the Home Secretary Joynson-Hicks, now pushed forward legislation to break the financial links between the trade unions and the Labour Party and to ban political strikes. In June the cabinet's legislation committee proposed a Trades Disputes Act that would do this. What is significant is the scale of opposition both within the Cabinet and among employers. Baldwin himself supported it. His reasoning, at least as given subsequently, was that the strike had strengthened the position of the Left and Minority Movement and legislation would assist the moderate leaderships. It was also noted that in these circumstances some trade union leaders might welcome provisions for secret ballots.[4]

In the Cabinet the main opponent was the Minister of Labour, Steel-Maitland. He was strongly backed by the Employers Confederation and by its president Lord Weir and the usually hawkish Engineering Employers' Association. A memorandum from the employers to the Minister of Labour in July warned of the dangers. It noted that while the trade union movement was 'somewhat disintegrated' it was likely to be reconstituted 'stronger than ever' and any hasty move to amend trade union law would be a 'mistake'. Until the situation was clarified 'no definite step should be taken by government [...] nothing would do more to consolidate the whole Trade Union and Labour Movement'.[5] Particular concern was expressed at the strengths of trades and labour councils, the main base for local trade union power during the general strike. 'Ill-considered action would strengthen the Labour Party'. The Engineering Employers proposed a Royal Commission to delay precipitate legislation.[6] Although there was no Royal Commission, the passage of the Trades Disputes Act was delayed for some months.

Also in June 1926, and with a parallel motivation, Steel-Maitland secured Cabinet agreement for an initiative to send a joint employer and trade union delegation to the United States to study that country's

3 *Lansbury's Labour Weekly*, 5 June 1926.

4 G.M. Young, *Stanley Baldwin* (Hart-Davis, 1952).

5 Glasgow University Business Archives (GUBA) Weir papers DC 096/16/26, July 1926.

6 GUBA Weir papers DC 096/16/14, 24 June 1926. Engineering Employers Federation.

industrial relations and its apparently thriving economy: 'methods adopted in that country may be brought under serious discussion in the settlement of our own problems'. No names were mentioned at this stage but it was likely that one leader Maitland had in mind was Ernest Bevin with whom he had worked closely both before and after the strike. The theme would be that of union–employer co-operation.[7]

Bevin Fights to Maintain His Authority

These months, May and June 1926, saw Bevin involved in frenetic activity to rescue the union and also his own reputation. His first intervention was in the London docks using his influence with the employers to get all grades back in employment on previous conditions. In this he mainly succeeded but at the cost of accepting a 'no-strike' clause and other concessions over the employment of strike-breakers. That done he travelled to his old base in the south-west to meet employers across the whole range of industries organised by the union. Here also employers insisted on no-strike clauses. In TGWU headquarters telegrams streamed in – over 80 in three days – reporting employers who were excluding strikers, the employment of scabs, demands for solidarity with other transport workers, such as rail workers who suffered much more systematic discrimination, and calls for continuing solidarity with the miners on the movement of coal.[8]

Telegrams also arrived from TGWU branches expressing anger at the way in which the strike had been called off.[9] Some were predictable – from the left-wing branches of the London dockers and bus workers and the Glasgow dockers (on whom a special file was opened after they demanded addresses of all other docks branches). More worrying were those from area secretaries reporting meetings in which votes to condemn the general secretary had either been passed or narrowly averted. An initial attempt to call together area secretaries in the week after the end of the strike was abandoned because of the wider chaos and rescheduled for 27 May. Bevin prepared meticulously for this meeting. A typewritten justification of his actions, 15 pages long, survives in the archives. It describes his part in trying to negotiate a settlement before the strike, his conduct during the strike and in even more detail the events resulting in the calling off of the strike.

The following week he wrote a letter to the chair of the Labour Party, Arthur Henderson. 'It is with considerable regret that I am driven to write to you that I cannot see my way clear to support the Labour Party and to

---

7   TNA CAB 24 180/35. Steel Maitland to Cabinet, 11 June 1926.
8   MRC MSS 126/TG/11/56.
9   MRC MSS 126/TG/11/1/36 and TG/11/1/55.

The Aftermath of the Strike

Summaries of Telegrams Received at TGWU Headquarters After the Strike Was Called Off – with Responses

MRC TG/11/56: It seems that the transcripts were made at a later date and the transcripts do not all follow time sequence

Date	Place	Comments
13 May 1926	Llanelly	Joint Strike Committee: no resumption of work; employers demanding reduction of wages and exclusion of certain workers
	Clyde	Meeting yesterday agreed to restart today and those not reinstated to sign strike roll. Since heard that Greenock Harbour Board and Port Glasgow Tramways and Railways only taking strikers back at discretion of managers. Will abide by decision of last night's meeting but if dockers and railwaymen decide to stay out keep away from rail stations and docks
	Cheltenham	Not a man returned to work solid as ever
	Leith	Employers refuse to resume work on old agreement. Decline to start work tomorrow
	Stockwell Mansfield Joint Transport Strike Committee	Mass meeting resolution: cannot accept conditions laid down by employer… several men and women employed by the railways and bus companies have been dismissed. No member shall sign on for further duty until assured every member shall return to former position
	Plymouth NUR TGWU General workers	Wholesale lockout prevails in Plymouth railways, docks and shipyards. Stoppage complete. Wire instructions
	Bromley ASLEF	Executive instructed members not to resume work until allowed to work unconditionally
	Bevin to Bromley	Our members instructed not to resume work until definite agreement
	Hornigold Kings Lynn	Conditions of railway re-employment unacceptable to men Our members called out in support wire instruction
	Bevin to Hornigold	You must not accept humiliating conditions. If men cannot return together they must stay out
	Fishguard	Marine Superintendent says supervisors cannot be re-instated: mass meeting unanimously refuse to return till all re-instated

Date	Place	Comments
	Bristol	Hill and Son Shipowners refuse to reinstate dockers and stevedores. Wire instructions
	Scunthorpe 10/25 branch Bro Hammerton	Members together with all other transport workers are pledged not to return to work until a promise of reinstatement has been given to all Transport workers
	Falmouth	Coastlines Ltd will not reinstate permanent men. Will you approach? Bevin wires Coastline: Executive has responded to PM's appeal in return to work. Suggest immediate meeting.
	Flour milling Green	Employees either not called out or have now returned or will be re-engaged. Bevin wires relevant officers that Secretary of Flour Milling Industrial Council states that any still on strike will be re-engaged
	Telford Avenue Bus Garage Area 1	Unanimous resolution from branch. No return to work till receive instructions from responsible official. Note: phone to Area 1
	Portsmouth	Railway carriers and municipal authorities refuse reinstatement. Dispute committee: remain out till satisfaction obtained
	Gloucester	Have tried to arrange return to work at timber yards. Timber Importers Association says they are not interested. Bevin: members must remain firm.
	Liverpool (Pugh)	Dockers resuming at old rates
	Cardiff (Bartlett)	This joint Rail Unions Strike Committee realising the tremendous revival of solidarity with the ranks of the strikers demand our respective ECs form a Joint Council of all unions who have members on strike for the purpose of carrying on fight to obtain status quo for all workers
	Workington (Cusack)	SS Florence loaded by blacklegs at Silloth. Hold up at Belfast. Sailing today.
14 May	Great Yarmouth	No return. Employers divided
	Jersey	Dockers have resumed work: no trouble experienced
	Southampton	Meeting with employers. Refuse general reinstatement.
	Falmouth and Penzance	All returned apart from Coastlines continuing to refuse reinstate: embargo placed
	Bristol docks	Will only neg if agree to working with blacklegs
	Chilcott	Employers agreeable to return on same terms as finished

Date	Place	Comments
	Newport	GWR claiming dislocation can not take on full complement.
	Stornoway	Interviewed employers. One declined to comment. Other said would take in all when present at 8 a.m.
	Dundee	Meeting employers. Old conditions. Will withdraw voluntary labour
	Grangemouth	Mass meeting: return on 1925 terms and dismissal of scabs
	Aberdeen	Dock employers post notices saying will re-employ on old terms
	Ayr	Ayr and Troon dock solid. Little work could be done without railway employers offer strike conditions
	Campbeltown	Situation quiet. Employers would accept previous conditions
	Greenock	Have met employers. Willing to restart old terms. Am holding up until trams agree to restart
	Bo'ness	Work suspended. Waiting instructions for meeting employers
	Workington	All ports working apart Barrow and Silloth which are railway docks and men refuse to sign forms presented by rail companies
	Kings Lynn	Our men not returning till railwaymen's conditions settled
	Hull	Met Port employers. Obnoxious terms. Cannot be accepted. Men standing firm other sections
	Boston	Boston Dock Company refusing to take back 18 permanent men
	Goole	Dock employers cooperating but men staying out in solidarity with rail workers
	Preston	Preston men resumed Thursday. No victimisation but work held up by rail strike
	Liverpool	Work resuming in docks on old terms apart from small firms in north end pending adjustments. Volunteers dismissed. Birkenhead and Garston not resumed: meeting Dock employers. Tramwaymen reinstated. Flour mill employers refuse to meet
	Plymouth	190 tramwaymen vote to return: old conditions; no victimisation
	Central Strike Committee, Tamworth	Three workers victimised by Midland Independent Bus Company. Bevin wires Crump Birmingham: take up

Date	Place	Comments
	Hull	Hull Corporation refusing to compromise on strikers. Could take up through National Joint Council
	Worthing	Southdown refuse to re-instate without victimisation. Wire instructions
	Hayle (Cornwall: Chinn)	Wire instructions at once
	Falmouth	Instructions wired. Statement regarding response to PL. Union will stand solid until satisfactory settlement reached
15 May	Mersey Dock and Harbour Board	Statement issued by Board wired (reinstatement but volunteers retained). Says meeting being held. Official Pugh says will recommend but will assure members that union will look after those not employed
14 May	London: LCCC and Combine trams	Instructions for a return to work. Staggered to avoid encounter with volunteers.
13 May	Worthing	Are we to resume work without prejudice? Bevin: previous conditions and no victimisation
	Bath	Bath tramways refuse to meet us. Rail men stand with us. Bevin Stand firm Await further instructions
	Silloth and Barrow	Ports imposing conditions. Men refuse unless status quo operates. Same conditions imposed on railwaymen.
	Croydon	Croydon Transport Advisory Committee has passed a resolution this morning asking every man to stand firm and not go into work
	Birmingham: Gleave and Crisp	Bevin: Moiley reached London this morning. All London tram and bus workers still out and standing solid. Circulate this to all BWO branches
	Swindon	All out Agreement not honoured by employers
	Belfast	Heysham and Fleetwood men not returned. Company refusing to take full staff. Meeting company. Meeting of men at 4,30. Wire instructions. Bevin: workers remain out as negotiations continue.
	Middlesborough	No return. Dock employers only offering day to day. Dockers will not return until black labour removed from rail jobs. Tramways not resumed.
	Lydney, Forest of Dean	Tinplaters refuse to return to work until victimisation of workers in all industries withdrawn
	Gloucester	300 men in coal yards still out
	South Wales	Docks still idle, men refused work in all docks, tramways and buses apart from Swansea

Date	Place	Comments
	Carlisle	Management refuse return on conditions; standing solid against
14 May	Liverpool	Railway Co at Garston refuse to dispense with men taken on during strike. Bevin stand firm No return
	North Western area	Regional Strike Committee calls on Executives to give permission for members to stay out on strike, 'No reply'
	Leyton Trades Council	All members of the TGWU shall be withdrawn till all allowed to return unconditionally. 'No reply'
	East Ham Trades Council and Council of Action	Call on all union executives to act together in face of employers. Please forward response to all Councils of Action 'No reply'
14 May	Wire from Bevin to 34 officers (responsibilities not specified)	Agreement reached. Members instructed to report forthwith
	Richards Plymouth	Reports on discussions with dock employers: all men to be taken back; men taken on during dispute to be dismissed. Bevin: accept. Return to work
	Hart, Waterford	Query: heard dispute settled; should ships be released. Bevin wire to Gillespie Dublin. Instruct in accordance our telegram
	Copenhagen Lyngate	Query: shall stop loading victuals for England. Bevin contact ITT
	Ward Strike Committee Cardiff	Calls on EC to approach rail unions for joint policy on crisis. Bevin: in close contact rail unions
	Grangemouth: Pearson	Local employers forcing free labour into local agreements. Bevin: stay out. Resist.
15 May	Bevin to all Reg secs	Complete reinstatement secured by NUR and ASLEF. All members should report for work
14 May	Hull	Flour millers agreed return previous conditions. Tramways and electricity holding up resumptions
	Swansea	Flour millers restarted previous conditions
	Manchester	Flour Mills at Coop resumed on satisfactory conditions. Private millers impossible strike continues
	Hull (Farmery)	Very few men have returned to work – exceeded by number who have been involved in new disputes. Number of strikers in ports in this area increasing
	Hull (Farmery)	Hull Corporation refuse to reinstate strikers
14 May	Assistant Gen Sec to Bro Clay	Make it known to London office that common arrangements made with rail unions
14 May	Nottingham	Tramway authority. Full return

Date	Place	Comments
	Birmingham	Birmingham Corporation Tramways Intervention with Lord Mayor has secured settlement with no penalty
	Midland Red Omnibus	Meeting of members voted to stay out – but most of those at meeting returned the following day. Only Committee (20) remain out. But some outlying garages still holding and local officer visiting all garages to hold.

13 May GENERAL AREA REPORTS	
Area No 2	Report from Hillman Met Dock Employers. No automatic reinstatement. Said no resumption of work. Channel Isles: Employers demanding impossible conditions Jersey All members have returned to work except 12 who return Monday Weymouth Employers refusing full reinstatement. Men out Bournemouth 260 tramway out: Tramway Committee met. No knowledge of outcome Reading Carting firms have agreed to reinstate. Pickfords demand non-union form. 900 tramwaymen still out Portsmouth All out. Committee refuses to reinstate 123 tramwaymen Isle of Wight No return Employers seeking to impose conditions Poole Employers have cancelled all agreements. No return. Southampton Employers demanding that foremen sign commitments. Strike continuing till condition dropped
Area No 3	Bristol. Met Employers Labour Association. Will not talk unless unions withdraw statement that no resumption if volunteer labour continued – refers to docks only. Further meeting being held. Employers Assoc covers docks, carters, warehouse, most grist milling. Lysaghs prepared to take back workers in galvanising. Alkali demanding new contracts. Lysagh's construction bound by Engineering Employers terms. Workers told to stand firm.
Area No 4	Only workers returning with conditions safeguarded are copper workers and tramway employees. Meetings required with rest
Area No 6	Manchester and Salford trams resumed today on old conditions. Docks: employers putting up impossible conditions; meeting of dockers has rejected. Manchester Ship Canal have offered old terms but men staying out as railworkers have not taken position yet.
Area No 8	Middlesbororugh dockers staying out in solidarity tramwaymen. Further meeting. Silloth and Workington. Negotiations proceeding

13 May GENERAL AREA REPORTS	
Area No 10	Hull employers have sought to force volunteers. Refused. Grimsby Employers seeking deregistration Goole seeking to limit registration Boston Seeking discharges and work with non-union King's Lynn Employers seeking end of existing agreement Immingham Governed by Grimsby conditions No resumption has taken place at any of the ports.
Area No 11	All members in Ireland returned to work on old conditions. Railwaymen still on strike
Area No 12	Fleetwood All out. Employers using volunteers Reston All returned Birkenhead Men refuse to return till all railwaymen settled Preston All returned Liverpool Coastwise Association All returned. Volunteers sacked Mersey Dock and Harbour Board Meeting today to consider position Rea's Tugowners. Seek reduction. Remain out Garston Still Employers employing volunteers Millers Still out. Will not meet union Trams running. 1,000 victimised. Sexton seeing Lord Mayor

take any part in its propaganda as long as Mr JR MacDonald is its leader'. He gives a list of MacDonald's betrayals including the use of emergency powers against the dockers and his validation of the forged Zinoviev letter. These he is prepared to overlook – but not MacDonald's attacks on the trade union movement's conduct of the General Strike. And he notes that throughout he himself held to a position that the strike 'must not be allowed to overthrow the constitution or to get out of control'.[10]

The previous week, the last week of May, had seen Bevin re-engage with Steel-Maitland and Horace Wilson in their efforts to secure a deal with the miners. He acted as go-between with the miners in an initiative also involving Lord Weir of the Employers' Confederation. As power supplies continued to be blocked, the employers urgently needed a quick settlement. So did the government – now including Churchill – desperate to get exports moving to sustain the pound. And so did Bevin. As long as the lockout continued a significant number of his members would remain out of work and, politically still more difficult, the TGWU would be subject to calls for solidarity action to support the locked-out miners by halting coal imports.[11] The initiative failed in face of the obduracy of

10 MRC MSS 126/EB/GS/7/44. Bevin to Henderson, 4 June 1926.
11 Bullock, *Life & Times of Ernest Bevin*, I, p.351.

the mine owners, still determined to enforce reductions and to do so on a district-by-district basis to break the national unity of the union. This left Bevin with major political, organisational and financial problems as he prepared for the executive meeting on 7 June.

The union faced a financial crisis. A surplus in January had been turned into an £300,000 deficit after expenditure of £600,000 during the strike and its immediate aftermath. Permission had to be secured to raise a loan and to impose a 6d a week levy on all members. Meantime the union was facing demands from the miners for solidarity action. As imported coal started arriving at the ports, at least some TGWU members were demanding solidarity action to stop it. And finally there was the associated political challenge from the Left condemning the actions of the General Council and hence also Bevin.

The minutes of the TGWU Executive show it posed no serious challenge to Bevin even though its elected members were likely to demonstrate more independence than area secretaries. Bevin defended the decision to call the strike – and also to call it off. He used the financial crisis to warn of the dangers of further solidarity action, referring back to the experience of 1921. He stressed that the immediate task was to restore all national agreements and get all members back into work.

He set out his position in the May–July 1926 issue of *The Record*, the first to appear for three months and also celebrating the first stage in the construction of the TGWU's new headquarters.[12] He defended the strike and continued to uphold the political use of strike action.

> We have lived through a wonderful period and we can have no regrets. We believe the struggle was inevitable; that the challenge had to be accepted; and whether it was conducted wisely or not the fact that stands out in bold relief is that the great bulk of the people were loyal, prepared to make sacrifices in the common interests.

He then launched an implicit attack on Thomas's treachery:

> Was it a failure? I say most emphatically No. Yet among those who are saying it was a failure are some of the very people who brought to us the Report of the Samuel Memorandum and recommended it to us as the triumphant result of the strike.

He ended by noting that in terms of changing policy it might have been better to have struck against the restoration of the gold standard itself and its consequences for the wages of all workers and the general economy. Nonetheless, the strike itself had resulted in a 'NEW ALIGNMENT

---

12 *The Record*, May–July 1926.

Victimised Women Workers Fight Back at George Kemp Ltd, Biscuit Manufacturer, Caledonian Road, London N7

Figure 7: Ornamental biscuit tin advertising Kemp's biscuits

Credit: The National Museum of Wales

George Kemp Ltd employed over 1,000 workers at its Caledonian Road biscuit factory in 1926. Apart from some male engineers, almost all were women. Shortly before the General Strike, Mary Carlin, TGWU national organiser, held factory gate meetings and managed to recruit over 150. As catering workers, they were not called out in the 'first wave' but by Wednesday 5 May pickets were on the gates and at midday power supplies were halted. The management told the workers to go home and to return on Friday to receive any payments due. On Friday, after standing in the rain for two hours, they were given two day's pay – and also their cards. That afternoon 700 of Kemp's workers signed on at the Tottenham Labour Exchange.

The morning after the strike ended, the TGWU members presented themselves for work. They were taken to the manager's office and asked why they had joined the union. They were then told to return the following Thursday.

Mary Carlin's report to the union EC, pleading for financial assistance, contains notes from one of the workers recounting what happened next:

We turned up on Thursday and found that those who did not join the union were working all the week and we were payed [sic] off with

notice stating not required which could mean anything. It was stated by Mr Whitehead that the 4 eyes cat [*sic*] of the Union woman had let you all down and those that did not join were still at work and you lot that has joined are still out.
[…]
Thursday May 20 went to City Road and on seeing Mr Hansen he said he did not know about the Kemp's people being organised and Mr Hansen phoned Mr Kemp and Mr Kemp was not a man to speak to Mr Hansen and he put the receiver back.

The note continues that Mr Kemp had spent £6,500 over the previous month on new machinery [about £6m in current values] which 'he's obtained out of the sweated labour of the girls picking up off the conveyer 46,000 biscuits per hour'.

Mary Carlin's report to the Executive asks for 'a very small sum' ('I know the position of the organisation financially') to encourage the sacked workers.

I had a terribly difficult task to persuade these workers to take their courage in both hands and join the Union as they knew Mr Kemp's attitude […] They were grossly underpaid. Now it is almost impossible for them to get other work […] They profess themselves anxious to stick with the union if I will stick to them and we have decided that a series of mass meetings outside of Mr Kemp's factory and a campaign in the newspapers will disturb Mr Kemp's equanimity and might have useful results.

Source: MRC MSS 126/TG/11/1/27.

OF FORCES' (capitals in the original text): 'The governing class of this country who, in the end, know how to retreat for safety, will be compelled by this great demonstration of unity to pay greater regard to the consequences of their policies than hitherto'.

At the 1926 TUC, a few weeks later, Bevin supported the General Council in thwarting Left demands to discuss the General Strike. Any discussion must be postponed until the miners' dispute was ended. He then took the lead in facing down a resolution from the miners calling for the General Council to be given more powers to require co-ordinated solidarity strike action.

The early autumn saw the high point of left-wing campaigning for solidarity with the miners and for retribution against those who were seen to have betrayed them. Led by *Lansbury's Labour Weekly* and backed by the Minority Movement, it sought to contest Ramsay MacDonald's call that the trade union movement should never again use strike action for political purposes. At the Labour Party conference the future Labour

Party leader George Lansbury argued that this shift of position would disarm working people and give power to their rulers. MacDonald himself had supported calls for strike action to stop war in 1914 and again in 1920. The German workers had used it to stop fascism in 1921. The Belgian workers had used it to win democracy. MacDonald's appeal for solely 'constitutional' action disarmed workers of their collective power and had, Lansbury argued, nothing in common with the traditions of Labour in Britain or internationally.

We do not know Bevin's position because by October 1926 he was already out of the country on the government organised deputation to the United States. The delegation to the United States was composed of two employers, two trade union leaders, a staff of civil servants and chaired by Sir William Mackenzie. It spent over two months in the United States and produced a lengthy report. During the visit Bevin also found time for a discussion with Lord Weir of the Employers' Confederation who happened to be in New York. Bevin was not overly impressed with US industry, was concerned at the weakness of its trade union movement and constantly annoyed his hosts by telling them that a serious trade depression was on its way.

Nonetheless, the discussions that started in the United States in October 1926 saw Bevin begin to develop new political horizons. At the end of the visit in November 1926 he sketched out the following wider options for British economic strategy in his notebook.

a. That Britain must have a customs union within the Empire, and

b. With Europe as well if possible

c. Or, if Colonies will not join, with Europe without colonies

d. That the associated manufacturers must meet Labour and review economic field with a view to raising consumer power of the population in the area mentioned above

e. That we must then in the industrial service mentioned above determine how to meet the demand at cost which will definitely raise the standard of living.[13]

These comments reflected Bevin's conviction that a good part of the dynamism of US industry depended on the continental size of its market. But they also seem to reflect a change in assumptions. They are no longer about how to secure a different type of society or even changing the balance of class forces in what existed. They are about how to use existing institutions, including the most repressive forms of colonial power, to maximise the market potential for British capital and to secure consequent benefits for labour.

13 Bullock, *Life & Times of Ernest Bevin*, I, pp.360–361.

Bevin Considers Political Dialogue
With the Employers – But Holds Back

As seen in previous chapters, Bevin had long experience of negotiations with employers. His strategy for building a general union had been to secure deals at national level with individual employers, like Mond's chemical combine or groups such as the flour millers, to end casualisation and win minimum conditions of employment – even though these deals often involved implicit or explicit agreements to minimise strike action. Both before the war and immediately after he had involved himself in Quaker-organised meetings for industrial peace and, during the war, had played a key part in government-sponsored joint boards for enhancing production (and workers' conditions). Yet none of these involved more wide-ranging discussions of national economic policy and international relations.

The 12 months following the general strike saw concerted efforts by the government and the Employers' Confederation to draw Bevin, along with a handful of other union leaders, into a far more political dialogue. As we have seen, these efforts were led by Steel-Maitland and his Permanent Secretary Sir Horace Wilson but had the backing of Baldwin and, from June 1926, of Cecil and Salisbury, and, very actively, of Lord Weir as president of the Employers' Confederation.

As soon as the delegation returned Weir made a speech in the Lords calling for a new era of co-operation between capital and labour. This was widely promoted in the press and had the active backing of Steel-Maitland and other Cabinet members. In early January Weir forwarded letters, originally drafted by Sir Horace Wilson, to Bevin, Kaylor of the Engineers, George Hicks and Arthur Pugh asking for a private meeting.[14]

At this stage, late 1926 and early 1927, the motivation of both government and the employers was fear of the growing influence of the Left. Still in November 1926 the great bulk of the million strong mining workforce remained loyal to its left-wing leaders. The memory of cities, towns and villages controlled by Councils of Action and strike committees was only six months old. On 22 November Steel-Maitland was warning the Cabinet that any precipitate anti-trade union legislation would politicise trade union members and play into the hands of the Left 'accelerating a process that has already begun'.[15] Four days later Robert Cecil was arguing the industry was 'permanently unsettled' and that further 'big disputes could

---

14 GUBA Weir Papers DC 096/1/108, Steel-Maitland to Weir, 22 November 1926, where he notes that Weir has 'had a general talk with Bevin' and asks him to make an initial approach when Bevin returns and also 'to have a go at Pugh'; and 096/1/109, Wilson to Weir, 5 January 1927, in which he says letters should be marked 'personal'.

15 TNA CAB 24 182/17 Steel Maitland to Cabinet, 22 November 1926.

be expected'.[16] This mood also affected the attitudes of the centrist trade union leaders.

In January 1927 Steel-Maitland wrote a further assessment explaining why the initiative for talks had, at least temporarily, been postponed at the request of the trade union side.[17] His comments are revealing. He noted the current interventions to curb communist influence, the very well-funded and publicised anti-communist crusade led by the right-wing leader of the seafarers union, Havelock Wilson, the establishment of a breakaway union from the MFGB in the Nottinghamshire coalfield and attempts at similar intervention in Yorkshire. But he doubted their effectiveness. 'The Minority Movement remains very strong'. The Communist Party, it was known, had doubled its membership to over 10,000 and trade union leaders, however cooperative, had to fight political battles against the Left inside their own unions and repair the organisational and financial damage inflicted by the General Strike.

He also posed a more fundamental question that takes us to the heart of the government's strategy. While there was a will on the part of trade union leaders to engage in dialogue, they were hesitant about its terms. Their unions were affiliated to the Labour Party. That party's aims were explicitly socialist and their members supported those aims. 'Before the TUC could go to such a meeting it would have to decide a number of questions that are very much at issue amongst its members [...] is the TUC to go on with its anti-capitalist campaign and demand the abolition of capitalism or is it to accept the existing system and see what are the best arrangements?'

The meetings which Steel-Maitland and Weir had in mind would need to be about 'the best arrangements' within the existing system. That was the point of the new dialogue. It was about changing assumptions – not necessarily about any detailed outcome. The fact that such discussions took place on these terms, publicly and formally, would be enough.

'Bevin in Particular Has a Great Many Rather Difficult Points in Front of Him'

How far this assessment of the difficulties facing the trade union side came directly from Bevin is unclear. Correspondence from Horace Wilson to Weir at the end of December 1926 indicates that substantial discussions had taken place. Wilson reports that 'Bevin in particular has a great many rather difficult points undoubtedly in front of him – some of which may

16 TNA CAB 24 182/29. Robert Cecil to Cabinet, 26 November 1926.
17 TNA CAB 24 184/28. Steel Maitland to Cabinet, 22 January 1927; Bevin had replied to Weir on 14 January 1927 'it would be much better if we postponed the acceptance of the invitation for the time-being', MRC MSS 126/EB/IP/1/7.

have an influence on his attitude'.[18] It was only after overcoming these difficulties, nine months later in autumn 1927, that Bevin was ready to move.

What were these difficulties? One was membership loss. At the end of 1926 the TGWU was losing members fast: 40,000 in the course of six months – over 10 per cent of the total and twice as many as the movement as a whole. The other was the anger of the membership – with at least one major attempt to form a breakaway union – and the demoralisation of full-time officers. Bevin addressed the 1 January New Year Dinner in Area 1 (London and East) thus:

> I regret the difficulties that you have had to pass through recently but I will confess that ever since I have been General Secretary until today I don't think there has been a month gone by without I have been threatened with a split from one part or other of this union. I am glad it has come to a test. Not merely has it come from the Dockers sections, it has come from several sections.[19]

Bevin was referring to the attempt to establish a new union by the London dockers, the National Union of Transport and Allied Workers, with, Bevin seemed to indicate, some support from the Transport Workers Federation. It was led by Fred Thompson and other dockers' leaders who had been to the fore in the 1923 unofficial strike and who had been strongest in their denunciation of the betrayal of the miners in May 1926 and subsequently. The attempt had been made while Bevin was in America and had only been thwarted by the detailed mobilisation of the union's officers from across the country.

Still in 1927 the issue of the miners' lockout and the union's failure to mobilise solidarity remained live. The miners had effectively been starved into submission just four weeks before. Bevin now addressed this issue. But he did so in a new way. 'After six months reflection [...] I still believe we did the right thing'. Now, however, the 'right thing' was not the decision to back a General Strike but the decision to call it off. 'I feel the General Council has nothing to be ashamed of.' And in an effort to cover himself from another angle of attack he went on to distance himself from Weir, Lithgow and Mond and the Employers' Confederation, attacking their opposition to the 48-hours agreement and declaring that he did not favour an industrial conference of the type they proposed.

The following four months saw Bevin making detailed visits to virtually every section of the union, addressing meetings and holding discussions with local officials. In February he convened a weekend meeting of 250

---

18 GUBA Weir Papers DC 096/1/109. Wilson to Weir, 29 December 1926.
19 *The Record*, January 1927, pp.66–67.

union officers and executive members at Shortnells, a stately home in south-east London, for three days of informal discussions. By July Bevin was ready to face the membership at the biennial conference in Swansea. A motion had been tabled by the Glasgow dockers branch (7/31) which deplored the attitude of the Executive Council in endorsing the action of the TUC in calling off the General Strike as 'a gross betrayal of the whole working class'. This 'unconditional surrender', it said, had led to 'wholesale victimisation'. The motion was defeated. So also was the motion from another Scottish branch (7/23) calling for the resignation of the union's representatives to the TUC for agreeing to the General Council's decision.

The conference then turned to the issue of the exclusion of communists from representing TGWU branches as delegates to local Labour parties and to trades councils. Fourteen London branches had motions opposing this exclusion along with two from Scotland and one from Area 6, Lancashire.[20] All were declared defeated. Bevin followed this by winning conference to reverse the rule decision made at the 1925 Scarborough conference which enabled executive power to be handed over to a central authority, the TUC General Council, for purposes of conducting national strike action.

Bevin's authority, after a difficult six months, was, at least formally, re-established. At the TUC conference in Edinburgh in September 1927 he played the leading role. He moved the General Council motion attacking the government's Trades Disputes Act now finally passed into law. But he also backed Citrine, the general secretary, in calling for the dissolution of the Anglo-Russian Joint Council established four years before to discuss issues of mutual concern with the Russian trade unions.

Perhaps most significant of all, Bevin moved the TGWU resolution calling on the trade union movement to develop wider political and economic perspectives that included strategic issues of national policy on current economic challenges. He gave a detailed analysis of the dynamism of the US economy in terms of its massive area and population and went on to call for a similar market to be created in Europe. The only solution is to 'inculcate the spirit of a United States of Europe – at least on an economic basis, even if we cannot on a totally political basis'. On this he was unsuccessfully attacked from the Left by A.J. Cook, Figgins from the NUR and Tomkins of the Furnishing Trades Association.[21] Their argument was that in taking this position Bevin was setting aims for the trade union movement that diverted it from its socialist objectives. More specifically, its call for a European Union betrayed the movement's internationalism with an 'exclusive agenda'.

20 MRC MSS 126/T&G/1887/2. Report of the 1927 biennial conference.
21 Bullock, *Life & Times of Ernest Bevin*, I, p.380; *Sunday Worker*, 11 September 1927; *The Record*, September 1927.

On 18 October 1927, Steel-Maitland tabled a detailed report for the Cabinet, probably written by Horace Wilson, that assessed the TUC conference as marking a decisive turning point. Socialist objectives had been overlaid by practical concerns of immediate policy and a breach had been made with Russian trades unions. The Cabinet report highlighted and quoted at length the presidential address from George Hicks. This, it was noted, was a compromise document agreed after some amendments by the General Council. It set out the need for the movement to develop economic policy aligned to immediate issues and for this to be done in partnership with employers at industry level. The report noted the inclusion of the phrase 'for this transitional period' to appease those who felt the proposal compromised the movement's long-term socialist objectives.[22]

The 1927 TUC did therefore mark a turning point and was seen to have done by the government. It did not explicitly abandon socialist objectives but overlaid them with much more immediate pragmatic goals that had very little to do with socialism. The ground was now set for the Mond–Turner Talks. In this process Bevin had played a major role.

22 TNA CAB 24 188/45.

7

'Mondism': Talking to Big Business 1927–28

In which Bevin champions industrial trusts

Discussions Finally Begin

Very shortly after the TUC's 1927 Edinburgh conference Lord Weir again sought discussions.[1] This time it was to be between TUC's General Council and a group of 20 major industrialists led by Alfred Mond, head of the giant Imperial Chemical Industries and now ennobled as Lord Melchett. Before undertaking the initiative Mond and Weir had unsuccessfully sought to win support from the two dominant employers' associations, the Federation of British Industry (which dealt with economic policy issues) and the Confederation of Employers' Associations (which dealt with labour relations). At this stage neither organisation was willing to commit itself – an indication perhaps of how far employer assessments of the labour situation had changed since the summer of 1926 and also, more definitely, of the strategic divisions in their own ranks. Privately Weir wrote to another member of the group, Sir Hugo Hirst, head of General Electric, saying he was nervous: 'we are walking on very thin ice'.[2] On the other hand, the leadership of the TUC, after its political victory at Edinburgh, was now keen to enter discussions, Bevin particularly.

After a preliminary dialogue on agendas, the two sides met formally, and with lavish publicity, in the premises of the Royal Society in Burlington

---

1 MRC MSS 126/EB/IP/1/7. Weir to Bevin, 19 September 1927; MRC MSS.126/ EB/IP/1/7. Bevin to Weir, 30 September 1927 would have 'a general discussion'; and Weir to Bevin, 3 October 1927 'will arrange by phone'.

2 GUBA Weir Papers DC 096/1/113. Weir to Sir Hugo Hirst, 26 December 1927.

House on 12 January 1928. A further meeting on 21 March 1928 determined a list of priority issues. Discussions continued on a weekly basis through the summer and autumn of 1928 with a succession of mutually agreed statements.[3]

The group of industrialists included a number with whom Bevin had negotiated recognition agreements over the previous years. These included Lord Ashfield who had a virtual monopoly of London transport, A.E. Humphries of the flour millers, McGowan of Imperial Chemical Industries and Hirst of General Electric and the National Grid. Most headed very big concerns that saw the future in terms of industrial rationalisation. Most had already themselves reaped the benefits of monopoly control in their own sectors.

Bevin's papers for the talks contain just one briefing document. It is a monograph on 'Present Day Tendencies in Industry' from Dr W.H. Coates, previously a senior civil servant and now adviser to ICI. Coates elaborated the then fashionable thesis that the development of large-scale industrial trusts, and the separation of management from ownership, produced 'a new broader outlook [...] a more exalted spirit [...] a deeper humanity. It may be expressed in one word "service"'. Bevin himself argued somewhat similarly on the more progressive attitudes of big employers in the January 1928 *Record*: 'it has been known for some considerable time that there has been a big conflict of opinion in the ranks of the employers as to the wisdom of the policy that has been followed since 1921'. Some of 'the very big interests' were seeking a different path and 'dare to make a move to meet Labour'.

The minutes of the meetings show that it was Bevin, usually with the support of Mond, who led discussions and often did so in meticulous detail. Issues covered included unemployment insurance, the compensation of workers made redundant through rationalisation, trade union recognition and the wider, more technical issues of economic and monetary policy, particularly on the adverse effects of the gold standard and the restriction of credit by the Bank of England.

A key theme was the need for industrial rationalisation. Bevin backed it – seeing it as essential if Britain was to compete. But he also insisted on the need to tackle labour displacement. On 8 November 1928 Bevin described a meeting he had had earlier the same day in an industry where 'probably [...] in the course of the next two years he would have the whole of the craft side wiped out by new machinery. He thought that to compete with America and Germany they had to do it. What could they do for these men?'. There was consensus that something should be done. Mond 'agreed with Mr Bevin and thought it was a national problem [...] The

---

3 The following account is based on the Bevin papers MRC MSS 126/EB/TU/5/1–10 and the Weir Papers GUBA DC 096 16/32.

whole country benefited by better production' and it should be the nation, not individual firms or workers, that should bear the cost.[4]

Ultimately, the discussions led nowhere. The detailed policy papers failed to secure any wider endorsement. As Weir feared, neither of the two employers' associations could be persuaded to enter directly into the discussions. A meeting of the Grand Council of the Federation of British Industries considered the issue in July 1928. Mond argued that as a result of the discussions TUC now supported the 'abandonment of class war and communist political trade unionism'. Sir Eric Geddes, reflecting the position of the traditional (non-rationalised) export industries, expressed scepticism. It was agreed to do no more than receive the reports and confer with individual associations.[5] Eventually on 13 February 1929 the president of the federation, Lord Ebbisham, replied that the discussions were not within the remit of his organisation. He did agree to meet the TUC General Council but very little came of it.[6]

The Politics of Industrial Peace

So what was the point? For Mond and his colleagues it certainly enabled them to broaden the base of support for policies which required, in their own business interests, greater state intervention, looser monetary policy and possibly a switch from the gold standard to a managed currency. As in Sweden, where such policies were adopted in the 1930s, the big trade unions were obvious partners.[7] For Bevin and at least some of his trade union colleagues, the logic was the same. The weight of big business support strengthened their challenge to the monetarist orthodoxies that then gripped the leadership of the Labour Party. Very early in the process the TUC side had organised a special briefing meeting that included Snowden, Dalton and Labour Party economists.[8] And additionally there was the more implicit benefit of bringing them very close to the men whose commitment to union recognition – though usually with 'no-strike' qualifications – was critical for the survival of their financially precarious organisations.

4 GUBA Weir DC 096 16/32. Transcript for 8 November 1928 meeting.

5 GUBA Weir DC 096/116/42. Minutes of the Grand Council 11 July 1928.

6 As above: Lord Ebbisham, 13 February 1929.

7 James Fulcher documents similar but more successful discussions in Sweden in the 1920s and 30s where industrial ownership was far more concentrated ('Labour Movement Theory Versus Corporatism: Social Democracy in Sweden', *Sociology*, 1987, vol.18, no.1, pp.252–262).

8 MRC MSS 126/EB/TU/5/5/4 contains Bevin's handwritten notes on the meeting on 27 March 1928: Snowden appears to have argued that gold standard did not hold back credit. The Mond Committee 'Memorandum on Gold' took an opposing position.

For the government the talks were also very important – even though Baldwin was happy to disregard the findings. The highly publicised meetings validated its policy of 'industrial peace' and completed the process of ideological realignment within the trade union movement. The focus of TUC policy was no longer, as it had been just three years before, on nationalisation. It was now rationalisation and managing it, jointly with big business, in the most humane fashion. It was a shift that in turn required the big unions to confront and defeat the remaining adherents of 'rank-and-file' socialism.

The turning point came at the 1928 TUC Congress. The Left had chosen the TUC's initiation of the Mond–Turner talks as its key target. The miners leader A.J. Cook had formed an alliance with the ILP to advance an alternative agenda based on socialist nationalisation, and targeted the talks in a pamphlet entitled *Mond Moonshine* – a position also endorsed by the Minority Movement and the Communist Party. At Congress the General Council had tabled a motion calling for endorsement of the talks. Cook opened the debate with an impassioned 30-minute speech and was supported by J.B. Brownlee and A.B. Swales of the engineers and George Hicks of the furniture workers. Their amendment simply urged caution. They cited in particular Mond's expressed admiration for Italian Fascism as a model for the new corporate state.

Bevin concluded the debate for the General Council. The talks, he said, were not an innovation but the outcome of other conferences. He wanted to know 'what the opponents of the report disliked whether it was Lord Melchett's religion, his race or his face. Cannot we proceed by discussion as well as starvation [...] the trade unions' part in this was not inspired by industrial peace or class collaboration but by a determination to assert for trade unions a new status and influence?' Trade union block votes assured a resounding defeat for the amendment: 3,000,000 to 500,000.[9]

Earlier in the Congress the General Council had voted to dissolve the Anglo-Russian Trade Union Committee and pressed forward its campaign to isolate the left-wing associated with the Communist Party. It secured backing for an investigation into the activities of communists and 'all those closely associated' with them or with the Minority Movement. Opposition from Arthur Horner of the miners and Tompkins of the furniture workers was heavily defeated. The following day the *Daily Herald* devoted a whole page to the 'Communist Conspiracy' and its alien ideology.[10] The Minority Movement's *Sunday Worker*, on the other hand, described the Congress as marking 'the greatest victory that the capitalists have yet achieved over the working class'. It would, it claimed, lead to the Labour Party forming a parliamentary alliance with the Liberals on non-socialist

9   *Daily Herald*, 4 and 7 September 1928.
10 *Daily Herald*, 4 and 5 September 1928.

terms (a general election was due to take place in 1929). A couple of weeks later the Labour Party National Executive extended its purge of the left to any members of constituency parties 'known to be associated' with the Minority Movement.[11]

In the September issue of the *Record* Bevin sought to explain his position to members. He challenged the Left's claim that talking to employers helps 'stabilise capitalism and prevents the development of socialism'. It was the task of the political movement to work for change. 'the trade unionist in his industrial capacity has to deal with the problems day by day [...] and has to decide whether to strike with all its attendant suffering or deal with the matters rationally as they arise through negotiation'. The trade unions were not entering 'some unholy alliance' but have 'taken the line that there is nothing coming within the realm of industry that should be left out of discussion'.[12]

Coping With Decline

In pursuing this policy of rapprochement with big business Bevin would have been acutely aware of the TGWU's own financial crisis and its declining membership. The recruitment campaign initiated after the Shortnells conference had reduced the rate of decline – helped in part by the recovery in employment levels in 1927. Whole sections, however, remained depressed. According to trade reports in the *Record* for 1927, tinplate continued at 40 per cent of previous levels, most dock employment dependent on coal exports remained depressed, particularly in Scotland, and the position in flour milling was described as 'very unsatisfactory'. In 1928 unemployment again rose. By then TGWU membership had fallen to just 316,000, 60,000 lower than it had been in 1925, lower even than it had been in 1927. Falling levels of trade, reduced dock and road transport activity and the pace of industrial rationalisation all took their toll. The *Record* gives details, among other industries, of compensation payments received by power workers as Sir Hugo Hirst's National Grid bought up and dispensed with obsolete local power stations.

Each of these statistics, of workplaces closed and members lost, conceals human stories of families on the breadline and a desperate search for work that often took people far away from their own communities. Employers were able to take full advantage – with women workers often the most vulnerable. Mary Carlin, the union's women's officer, reported in 1927 on shop assistants in Cornwall being paid just ten shillings (£0.50p) for a six-day week and then being discharged and replaced by still cheaper

---

11 *Sunday Worker*, 4 and 11 September 1928.
12 TGWU *Record*, September 1928.

and younger women – at a time when unemployment pay itself was 50 per cent higher at 15 shillings (£0.75p).[13] However, she also reports other instances where women were collectively fighting back and how a mainly female workforce at a factory in Bermondsey came out en masse over the sacking of a woman shop steward. The firm was forced to agree to a joint committee of workers and directors to arbitrate in future cases.[14]

The late 1920s were therefore difficult times for both the union and its members. Falling membership meant reduced income for a union that had borrowed massively to pay benefits during and after the General Strike and still had to meet the costs of its new headquarters, Transport House, which finally opened in March 1928.

It was in these circumstances that Bevin began discussions about amalgamation with the Workers Union following an informal approach by its officers in November. Formed by Tom Mann in 1898, the WU was the third biggest of the general unions, reaching a membership of over 300,000 by 1920. With the onset of mass unemployment in 1921 its membership collapsed. By 1927 membership was only a little over 100,000 dispersed over a wide range of industries. The union had low membership fees and paid high benefits and additionally carried a very large staff of full-time officers, over 100, to service its widely scattered membership. It may also have been in some difficulty politically. The Minority Movement's *Sunday Worker* gives considerable coverage to reported financial irregularities in the early months of 1927 and reports the Left as winning a ballot calling for the resignation of six executive members.[15] Cumulatively these problems appear to have been the trigger for the union's approach to Bevin.

Discussions continued until terms for a merger were agreed in the autumn of 1928. Details were sent out to members of both unions in December 1928. Over three days in the week before Christmas, 18 membership meetings were held across the country with Bevin speaking at many of them. He wrote in the December *Record*: 'amalgamations of capital must be met by amalgamations of labour [...] unity is essential if we are to keep up the pace set by economic development [...] the trustification of industry, interlocking, accumulating and controlling interests creating problems which must be faced by every individual worker'. The Workers Union, despite its weaknesses and its immediate crisis, had important concentrations of members in engineering and electrical trades in the West Midlands and London, and gave the TGWU a much firmer foothold in the types of expanding consumer industries represented by the Mond group of employers and hence a basis for extending its recognition agreements on an industrial basis. No less significant for the future, the union had a

13   *The Record*, April 1927.
14   *The Record*, February 1927.
15   *Sunday Worker*, 27 February 1927.

significant number of women members and women full-time officers. The successful ballot for amalgamation took place through the early weeks of 1929.[16]

By then the focus of the union and its members was on preparations for the forthcoming general election due in May 1929.

Bevin maintained a very ambivalent attitude to the Labour Party. He deeply distrusted its parliamentary leadership, MacDonald, Snowden and Thomas particularly. He disliked many of its new parliamentary recruits, ambitious careerists defecting from the Liberals. On the other hand, he saw it as 'his' party. His new headquarters, Transport House, provided headquarters for the Labour Party. He personally had a key role in the direction of its daily paper, the *Daily Herald*. The TGWU was the party's biggest single donor and he had waged a long campaign through 1927 and 1928 to combat the 'contracting in' provisions of the Trades Disputes Act and to ensure that all TGWU members individually subscribed to the party.

At the 1928 party conference he had expressed his dislike of the party's new programme *Labour and the Nation* as too long and high blown. His views were reflected in the much shorter election manifesto which focused on the actions that could be taken to combat unemployment – with the government actively creating jobs by financing infrastructure development.[17]

However, strikingly, the new manifesto made no mention of nationalisation or of socialism. In this it was in strong contrast to the manifesto launched jointly by the now semi-detached ILP and A.J. Cook. Instead the Labour programme looked forward to the benefits of large-scale but still privately owned rationalisation in transport, docks and energy provision. The government should regulate. It should not own. In this regard Labour's programme for government did reflect some of the perspectives of the Mond discussions.

16 Richard Hyman, *The Workers Union* (Oxford University Press, 1971), p.210.
17 Bullock, *Life & Times of Ernest Bevin*, I, p.416.

Concluding Comments

In 1938 Baldwin claimed credit for having transformed Britain's labour movement. As we have seen, his claim was not without justification. Over four short years the movement's assumptions, ideology and organisation had been drastically modified.

In 1925 Bevin and the TGWU, along with the rest of the movement, were committed to the immediate public ownership of key utilities and the medium-term objective of a fully socialist society. In achieving these objectives they saw the industrial power of working people as a key instrument. They understood this in class terms: that only the collective organised power of working people could combat the domination of private wealth. By 1928 these commitments had been abandoned by the leadership of both the TUC and the Labour Party – explicitly in terms of banning the political use of the collective strength of organised labour, implicitly at least in terms of socialism.

However, possibly still more damaging, was the way in which this had been achieved. It involved the successive exclusion and marginalisation of all who opposed – in the Labour Party, in the trades councils and to a large extent within trade unions themselves. By 1929 the united, cohesive rank-and-file-based movement that had emerged during the war, and that had been able to challenge the government in 1919 and defeat it in 1920 and 1925, was largely a thing of the past. Institutionally, the Labour Party was stronger – but no longer, as will be seen next, in terms of its coherence and the political vigour of its mass base.

And at each stage of the process Baldwin's hand, though well hidden, was active: first in ideologically dividing the movement before 1926 and, with cold calculation, enforcing the General Strike. Then, subsequently, with the movement weakened and vulnerable, setting up the discussions with employers that forced the TUC leadership to publicly justify its new policies of big business collaboration and industrial peace,

In a strange way Bevin himself seems to have been aware of this. Writing in 1927 he described Baldwin as 'designing'. 'the real Mr Baldwin is in perfect harmony with the diehards'. He 'created the set of conditions that made the national strike absolutely inevitable'. 'His record was one of betrayal'.[1]

However, it would be wrong to credit Baldwin with single-handedly shifting the balance of power within Labour. He had willing helpers. Much of the Labour Party leadership was only too happy to see the militant Left isolated. So also was the older generation of trade union leaders who had worked with the government during the war.

Nor did everything go Baldwin's way. None of his careful planning prepared him or his colleagues for the scale of response to the General Strike or the mass class mobilisation that did, at least for a short while, change assumptions about class power in towns and cities across Britain. In consequence, the government backed away from its planned general offensive against wages – ultimately making it far more difficult, and ultimately impossible, to stabilise the pound on the gold standard. Moreover, even Baldwin's programme of 'education' for Labour was not final. Despite the proscriptions and exclusions that followed, the experience of the General Strike was not forgotten. Within a decade a new generation was beginning to emerge.

1   *The Record*, September 1927.

Section II 1925–29

Questions for Discussion

- Did the government have an overall strategy during this period – and is it helpful or not for our understanding to talk about a 'ruling class'? If so, how is its operation best understood?

- Could the general strike have been won – both for the miners and the trade union movement in general? Was Bevin correct when he later commented that strategically it would have been better to have made the key demand a reversal of the return to the gold standard?

- In 1927 Steel-Maitland, the Minister of Labour, posed the question facing the trade union movement as follows: 'Is the TUC to go on with its anti-capitalist campaign and demand the abolition of capitalism or is it to accept the existing system and see what the best arrangements are?' Was this an accurate assessment of the key question facing the TUC and, if so, what implications did it have for government policy?

- Was Bevin correct in seeing the NMM and the post-1928 stance of the ILP as divisive? Alternatively, how far did his campaign against them in the union and the Labour Party prepare the way for the collapse of the second Labour government?

III

Rescuing Labour
1929–31

Introduction

*How Bevin rescues the Labour Party from disintegration in 1931
and calls for a great campaign of socialist education – but only after
Bevin himself had spent five years rooting out socialist influence in
the union and more widely in the Labour movement*

May 1929 saw the election of the second Labour government. This government was again without a majority but this time it had the biggest number of seats, 287. The Wall Street crash occurred four months later and two years after that, in August 1931, Britain's banks – overlent to failed banks in Germany and Austria – faced a run on their reserves. To restore confidence in sterling, the Bank of England and the Treasury demanded draconian cuts in public expenditure, in pensions, benefits and public sector wages. When MacDonald and Snowden sought to implement these cuts, the Executive of the Labour Party, mainly composed of representatives of the big unions, opposed. MacDonald, along with leading Cabinet members, abandoned the Labour Party, joined with the Conservatives and Liberals, and formed a national government. MacDonald then called a general election. Robbed of much of its parliamentary leadership, the Labour Party faced electoral disaster.

It was Bevin who was largely responsible for rallying the Labour Party in opposition to MacDonald and his demand for cuts. It was Bevin also who subsequently fought to save the Labour Party electorally. 'We are now entering the most gigantic political struggle that Labour has had to face and the outcome of the struggle will have a tremendous effect not only on the political outlook of the Nation but upon the standard of living, wages and conditions generally of the people [...] the Labour Party will win this election.'[1] In the event the national government won. Labour was reduced

---

1 TGWU *Record*, October 1931.

from 286 seats to 46 – even though the fall in its overall vote was less: from 8.0 million to 6.3 million.

After the election Bevin was defiant:

Socialists have nothing to fear [...] if we are to have a successful democracy we must have an intelligent one [...] I do not believe that the tactics used by our opponents can ever be successful again provided that the Labour Party now inaugurates a great educational campaign to secure for the electorate a better understanding of socialist principles and a more intelligent grasp of the economic laws of the present system.[2]

These traumatic weeks for Britain's Labour movement demonstrated both the strengths and weaknesses of Bevin and of the union which he had struggled to create over the previous ten years.

By 1931 the TGWU was Britain's biggest general union. Thanks to the amalgamation with the Workers Union it was now bigger than J.R. Clynes' General and Municipal Workers Union. Although smaller than the Miners' Federation, it had a political and organisational unity that the MFGB, and most other unions, lacked and was by 1930–31 stamped with Bevin's personal authority. Despite its size, its industrial diversity and the very differing origins of its component unions, Bevin's leadership was now (almost) unquestioned.

The union also provided the headquarters for both the TUC and the Labour Party and Bevin himself was largely responsible for the survival of the *Herald* as the party's daily paper. In 1930 he had relaunched it, jointly with Odhams Press, as a mass-produced commercial venture, with both London and northern editions and reaching a circulation of one million by the end of the year. This paper remained with the party in 1931 and was critical in maintaining its cohesion and mass support.

Bevin also exercised an intellectual dominance within the General Council of the TUC. He led most debates demanding any wider understanding of economic and financial issues and through 1930 and 1931 played a very active role in government commissions on issues of economic and financial policy.

Yet Bevin's own assessment after the 1931 election revealed the weakness in his own position and that of the Labour Party. He rightly identified the critical weakness of the Labour Party in the 1931 election as the lack of a wider understanding of what socialism was and how to achieve it – hence the need for a 'great educational campaign' for socialist principles.

Yet this immediately brings into question the policies pursued by Bevin and the union for the five years after the General Strike. Bevin had

2 TGWU *Record*, November 1931.

been a leading figure in the purge of the Left – not just communists but all those associated with the Minority Movement, probably up to a third of all trades councils and, in terms of registration at Minority Movement conferences, a very significant number of trade union branches, constituency Labour parties and individuals. These had been the bodies that mobilised local working-class communities in 1920, in 1925 and again in 1926.

By 1929 trades councils across Britain had been fully subordinated to TUC's Trades Councils Joint Consultative Committee (and the Scottish TUC's equivalent) that controlled agendas and actions. Those that did not follow these instructions were disbanded. Local Labour parties suffered similar restrictions and exclusions, particularly as the administrative separation of trades councils and Labour parties gathered pace. Some became the property of local political dynasties. Some sought to continue as local campaigning bodies. Only a few formed part of a cohesive local movement that could mobilise working-class communities as a whole. In the face of mass unemployment from 1929 onwards, contact was even banned with the main organising body for the unemployed, the National Unemployed Workers Movement.

It was also the case that Bevin's own union, both organisationally and in terms of the way it operated, tended to centralise decision-making and marginalise local shop-steward and branch activity. Although responsibilities were delegated to both areas and trade groups, authority was ultimately concentrated in the hands of the Executive and in practice largely exercised by Bevin and his senior officers. This in turn matched the pattern of the union's industrial relations. The TGWU relied on national agreements with major employers or groups of employers. Local disputes were not encouraged – and after the General Strike, when the new agreements often contained 'no-strike' clauses, tended to be actively prevented.

As we saw in Section II, these agreements also reflected the way Bevin increasingly saw economic development. Big combines and trusts could deliver better conditions and benefits. Bevin's promotion of the Mond–Turner talks tended, despite his caution, to create a belief in managerial solutions to problems of unemployment and poverty. In the set-piece debates at the TUC and the Labour Party conferences, Bevin was employed to denounce the utopian ideas of Cook and Maxton and the Communist Party.

Bevin was therefore right about the need in 1931 for a 'great educational campaign' for socialism. What had been a cohesive, community-based movement for working-class mobilisation, led by trades councils and Labour parties, and posing socialism fairly directly against capitalism, had by 1931 largely vanished. Bevin had played no small part in this.

The consequences were long term. The national government of 1931was re-elected in 1935. For a decade it was able to enforce anti-working-class policies. Wales, Scotland and the North suffered unprecedented levels of unemployment and industrial depression. Internationally, its policies were no better. The fact that Britain was somewhat less exposed to the effects of the collapse of world trade in the 1930s largely depended on its control of a massive empire market and the materials it produced: oil, rubber, copper and zinc. For the rich the benefits were massive: dividend payments from BP were running at 15 per cent for most of the decade. But for the colonies the collapse in producer prices brought hunger, resistance and repression. Moreover, and fatally, in terms of international relations, it tilted Britain's foreign policy towards alignment with Europe's fascist powers. In the face of fascist expansionism, the US and the Soviet Union proposed, from 1936, an anti-fascist alliance. Britain refused, in large part because in return the US required access to British empire markets. These policies led to the betrayal of the Spanish Republic and eventually to another world war.

This section will look first at the achievements of Bevin and the leadership of the TGWU in stabilising the union in a period of growing mass unemployment and industrial depression. It will then examine the role of the union, and particularly of Bevin, within the broader Labour movement and the relationship with the Labour Party. It will close by examining the debacle of August 1931 and Bevin's role in rescuing the Labour Party.

8

Running the Union in Difficult Times
Too Close to Employers?

In the face of the intensifying economic crisis from autumn 1929, the TGWU and its members probably managed better than most. Though all sections of the membership struggled with pay cuts and redundancies, the bulk of the union membership were in areas of the economy that were relatively sheltered. While steel, shipbuilding, coal and heavy engineering were savaged – with output collapsing by up to a third – passenger transport continued more or less as before. Docks and road transport, depending on locality, were harder hit, particularly in the north and west where there was greater dependence on heavy industry. The new consumer industries in the Midlands and South East, in electrics, cars and light engineering, continued to grow as import prices fell sharply and the middle class particularly gained greater purchasing power. On this front the merger with the Workers Union, based as it was largely in these newer industries, was particularly timely.

The Workers Union Amalgamation

Writing in the *Record* for July 1930, Bevin celebrated the amalgamation as 'successful' and having proceeded with no major problems. 130 full-time officers had been integrated into the structures of the TGWU and a new General Workers section established – the Metal, Chemical and Engineering Trade Group – into which a major part of the Workers Union membership was transferred. Previously, in December 1929, Bevin had drawn up a plan for the integration of membership and offices at area and trade-group level. The bulk of the new members were placed in the general trades group under Devenay of the TGWU and Dalgleish of the Workers Union.[1]

---

1 MRC MSS TG/1268/3. Scheme of Area Organisation and Central Administration December 1929.

In terms of area organisation the biggest change came in the Midlands. Here there were 22,000 Workers Union members as against only 14,000 in the TGWU, and it was here that the expanding motor, aircraft and consumer electrical industries were based. Other substantial concentrations of Workers Union members were in the North West (9,500), Yorkshire (7,800), the South West (7,500) and Ireland, mainly Belfast, with 6,800. The London membership was also big but dwarfed by the TGWU. Elsewhere, such as in Areas 8 and 10, Workers Union members only numbered a few hundred.[2]

Up until World War One the Workers Union had in large part been sustained by the activist philosophy of Tom Mann, within which members organised at plant level, protected their branch autonomy and where full-time officers were subordinated to branch decision-making (in Belfast its key full-timers had been pupils of Connolly). During World War One the banning of strikes and the requirement for executives and full-time officers to enforce government conditions transformed this relationship and created a centralised structure. In war conditions the union actively used its official standing to assert negotiating and membership rights across semi-skilled workers in the munitions industry and elsewhere. But its success terminated with the war. Unlike the TGWU, the union had few national agreements forged at industrial level and relied, unsuccessfully, on its large number of full-time staff, and its financially unsustainable high benefits, to maintain membership at plant level. Only in the Midlands, with its expanding consumer industries, did this strategy have some effect and here also, as in one or two other areas, particularly Ireland, the activist philosophy to some extent survived.

While TGWU membership had also contracted, as we have seen, the fall was much less precipitate than in the Workers Union. Bevin's carefully nurtured national agreements usually involved employers themselves encouraging union membership and even in some cases making it obligatory. Additionally, the TGWU made very good use of the JICs (Whitley Councils) established during the war to arbitrate matters of dispute, and Bevin was himself a supremely effective negotiator. This approach had the great advantage, as Bevin repeatedly stressed, of ensuring that there remained in Britain – despite depression and unemployment – a powerful organised voice to defend workers' interests both politically and industrially.

---

2 MRC MSS TG/1268/2. Workers Union Membership December 1929. Hyman, *Workers Union*, pp.150–158 details WU strengths by area in the early 1920s that roughly matches, though in general the Midlands membership seems to have held up best in face of the general membership collapse.

Industrial Peace or Collaboration? The Flour Milling Industry

Yet this approach also led to a passive membership. Full-time trade union officials saw it as their role to defend the agreements reached with employers, to maintain the existing hierarchies of pay and conditions, including those that fixed women in a permanently subordinate position, and in periods of contraction, such as after 1929, to co-operate with management in shedding capacity and jobs. Increasingly, therefore, trade union officers ran the danger of assuming a policing rather than mobilising role. Jack Jones in his autobiography vividly describes consequences in Liverpool's docklands in the early 1930s.

One prime example of this approach could be found in the flour milling industry which Bevin always held as an object lesson of employer–trade union partnership. Immediately after the war, in 1919, a Joint Industrial Council was established between Bevin's union, then the Dock Workers, and the combined employers.[3] For the following decade, Dr A.E. Humphries for the employers and Bevin for the union alternated as chairs. In 1928 both joined the Mond–Turner discussions. Back in 1921 Bevin had written to the membership to report on the consultation in favour of accepting a wage reduction: in the consultation 'there was of course a natural opposition to any reduction' but the course of events made it inevitable. 'If the organisation is not kept strong there is a danger of the whole position slipping back to that of 1919'.[4] This was always Bevin's fear, a not unjustifiable one. Organisation had to come first.

But by the end of the decade the relationship had become something more compromising. Both Bevin and Humphries were enthusiastic members of the Mond–Turner committee and held up 'their' industry as a model for others. Already rationalisation was well in progress. Flour milling, however, was not an industry that was particularly affected by international terms of trade or a slump in exports. Bread was always going to be needed and the import costs of grain were actually declining. Rationalisation was far more about monopolisation and profits. The Millers Mutual Association, financed by the biggest firms in the industry, was systematically buying up smaller, local and rural mills and closing them down. A leading firm among them was Joseph Rank, later Rank Hovis MacDougall, with which the TGWU had had a partnership agreement from March 1926, and where the benefits of monopolisation seem to have been enough to allow the owners to buy up a large slice of Britain's film industry and cinemas in the 1930s.[5]

3 MRC MSS 126 TG/RES/GW.31/1. National Joint Industrial Council for the Flour Milling Industry, 23 July 1919.

4 MRC MSS 126 TG/RES/GW/31/1. 'To the Workpeople in the flour milling industry from Ernest Bevin', 29 June 1921.

5 MRC MSS 126 TG/RES/GW/31/v. Agreements with Joseph Rank.

Bevin made use of the situation to negotiate benefits for his members: technical education, improved health and safety provision and one week's annual paid holiday. In his comments as chair of the Joint Council he made clear he was fully aware that profits were rising not falling. In the 1931–32 annual report he comments that the process of rationalisation had 'brought a fair harvest to those who had invested in it' and the year before he noted the prosperity of the industry.[6] But this investment was not in plant and machinery. It was to scrap it – and the jobs that went with it. The reports of the flour milling trade group for 1930–31 list ten mills closed in the three months to April 1930.[7] In some cases, but not all, payments were secured for those who lost their employment. Many, however, would have lived in areas where replacement employment would have been very difficult to find. Naturally also, given the relationship with the employers, no attempt was made to mobilise members for resistance to closures. The Joint Council's annual meetings themselves began to take on a cosy and self-congratulatory tone. In his annual statement to the Flour Millers Board in 1928, Bevin commented on the subject of employees' reluctance to wear the protective clothing supplied. This, he said, had something to do with the 'contempt of risk of the Anglo-Saxon mind [...] which was allied with the spirit of adventure and probably had a lot to do with the superiority of the Anglo-Saxon race' (and not presumably anything to do with the unsatisfactory character of the clothing).[8]

It is also clear from the repeated appeals from the two sides of the Council, issued jointly by employers and the union, for all workers to join the TGWU, that union membership was not just largely passive but that significant numbers were fading out and not paying union dues. It was this tendency to collude with management in the endorsement of the status quo, including its inbuilt injustices and inequalities, that may also have something to do with the mystery of female membership of the TGWU.

The Mystery of the TGWU's Female Membership

Some light is shed on this lack of reference to work among women by interviews which took place in 1938 conducted by the TUC with veterans of the trade union movement including two key organisers from the

6 MRC MSS 126 TG/RES/GW/31/1. Annual Report 1931–32. There are direct parallels here with the Woollen Industry's Joint Industrial Council where Ben Turner commented on 'cosy cooperation under stress': C. Wrigley, 'Cosy Cooperation under Stress', *Borthwick Papers*, No. 72, 1987.

7 MRC MSS 126 TG/131/D1/2. Reports and Minutes of the Flour Milling National Trade Group.

8 MRC MSS 126 TG/76/AR/2. Annual Report of the Joint Council 1927–28: Bevin speaking as chair (he alternated each year with Humphries).

TGWU: Mary Carlin and Julia Varley who joined in 1929 from the Workers Union. Both were remarkable women.[9]

Julia Varley had been born in 1870. She joined the Weavers Union in 1886 and had been active in the trade union movement ever since. There had been a radical tradition in her family and she remembered her grandfather, an old Chartist, talking to his former comrades about the struggles of the 1840s when the workers seemed about to take over the world. She also remembered the Manningham Mills strike in Bradford in 1890 as being the making of trade unionism among women, hitherto largely restricted to textiles in the north-west.[10] Between 1893 and 1899 she had been secretary of the Weavers Union and thereafter, up till 1914, had worked with Mary McArthur in the National Federation of Women Workers and joined the Workers Union during the war.

Mary Carlin criticised the position then existing in the TGWU: 'we have no women on our union executive, never had a special place for women. We have not been encouraged to bring women forward at all'. She was also critical of the wider strategy of relying on trade boards. 'Whatever benefits Trade Boards have bestowed on workers, they are a great snag to organisation'.[11]

Her exasperation, and that of the other female organisers, Julia Varley and Mary Quaile, comes across on occasion in their quarterly reports to the general trades. In 1930 Mary Carlin reported she had been trying to organise the women cleaners in ICI and deal with the poor working conditions encountered. 'I cannot report much progress and the General Secretary undertook to take this up with the firm. I believe the matter was raised but I have no information on any progress having been made'.[12]

It was only later in 1930, and in response to the initiative of the TUC to take steps to co-ordinate the organisation of women, that the union's General Executive Committee convened a conference of the women organisers of the union to give 'general consideration to the question of the policy to pursued within this union in seeking to organise women'.[13] In January 1931 the Executive responded to its recommendations by agreeing 'limited special expenditure' for carrying out organising campaigns in chosen districts. The same meeting also agreed to send Miss A. Arnold, Miss M. Carlin, Miss K. Manicorn and Miss M. Stewart to the conference

9 MRC MSS 292/10.2/17.2. Report on the Women Veterans Causerie, 4 July 1938. Trades Union Congress.
10 Julia Varley, 'Yesterday and Today', TGWU, *The Record*, March 1931.
11 MRC MSS 292/10.2/17.2. Report on the Women Veterans Causerie, 4 July 1938. Trades Union Congress.
12 Report of Mary Carlin to the General Trade Group MRC MSS 126/TG/807/1/1.
13 MRC MSS 126/TG/1186/A/8. Minutes of the General Executive Committee, 21 October 1930.

organised by the TUC for the organisation of women workers.[14] the following month the women's page of the *Record* reports the call from the TUC for trades councils and trades unions locally to jointly establish local organising committees for women workers. Again the initiative came from the TUC.

Some advances were made on other fronts and the amalgamation with the Workers Union secured a very considerable increase in the union's female membership and brought with it female organisers who subsequently took leading positions in the union. It was also this new female membership in the Midlands that was later responsible for a number of the key unofficial disputes in the early 1930s in the car industry. But the structural problem remained. Endorsing what existed in agreements with employers also endorsed existing structures of inequality and oppression.

Dissent, Expulsions and Unofficial Action

It is difficult to gauge the scale of dissent inside the TGWU in the years 1929 to 1931. By then the major challenge to Bevin's leadership from the dockers and bus workers in the immediate aftermath of the General Strike was a distant memory. Detailed work had been carried out in the following years to weed out and suspend branches affiliated to the Minority Movement and to remove TGWU affiliations from trades councils that remained affiliated to it such as that in Glasgow.

At the 1929 biennial conference, motions directly critical of the leadership's policies came from just 12 branches, nine in London and one each from the South-West, Wales and Scotland.[15] Two were against class collaboration through the Mond talks, two branches called for resistance to the monopolisation of London's bus services (and the TGWU's acquiescence), one for a general resistance to the capitalist offensive, two called for industrial unions and one for the establishment of works committees (a demand of the Communist Party), two (South West and Scotland) called for a commitment to use industrial action to halt a new war and two called for an end to the use of block votes at union conferences and the right of individual delegates to voice opinions. All were defeated.

Two years later at the 1931 biennial, a dozen branches again put in critical motions. One or two branches such as Cricklewood Bus reappear from 1929 but otherwise there was no continuity – and two Workers Union branches joined the opposition, one from London and one from the North West. This time there was condemnation of the Labour government's policy of repression in India, the call for a general strike against any war with the USSR, three praising the USSR's five-year plan and two opposing

14 MRC MSS 126/TG/1186/A/9. Minutes of the General Executive Council 13 January 1931: Minute No. 31.
15 MRC MSS 126 TG/1887/3/2. Final Agenda 1929 Biennial.

policies of industrial peace.[16] Finally there was one from the administrative staff at the Port of London (which Bevin privately described as 'treasonous' and for which the London area secretary personally apologised for failing to stop) which condemned the concentration of power in the hands of the general secretary.[17] Again all were defeated.

Some expulsions and suspensions had taken place meantime, particularly against members in London buses. In May 1929 the secretary of the Cricklewood branch, C.A. Drabwell, was suspended from membership and banned for holding office for four years. There also appears to have been disciplinary against some of the Workers Union branches in London during the amalgamation. Six branches, Shepherds Bush, Acton, City Packers, Kilburn, Barnsbury and Tottenham Hale, were suspended until they committed themselves 'not to take any steps to influence any delegate or delegates to violate the rules of the union'.[18]

Overall these branches constituted only a minute fraction of the total number of union branches across Britain and Ireland, although possibly significantly 'rebel' motions made up over a fifth of all those submitted to the biennial conferences in both 1929 and 1931. The great bulk of branches sent nothing.

Perhaps a truer reflection of the void opening up between the leadership and members may be found in the continuing level of often small-scale unofficial strike actions and protests provoked by the agreements negotiated by the union with particular employers and employers' federations and then locally policed by union officers.

In January 1930, in just four weeks, three unofficial strikes are recorded. The biggest was at the food processing firm Crosse and Blackwell in Bermondsey where the management had sacked eight men and replaced them by women workers, but at women's rates. The entire workforce of 1,000 women and 200 men came out to demand reinstatement. They were ordered back by the TGWU which had an agreement with the firm dating back to March 1926 covering its plants in Silvertown, Bermondsey and Dundee. When the workers refused, the union for a brief period made the strike official but again withdrew support (and strike pay) and eventually the workers returned on the management terms without reinstatement.[19]

In Swansea there was an unofficial strike at Patent Fuels reported on 10 January against a wage reduction agreed by the TGWU and the same

16 MRC MSS 126/TG/1887/3.

17 MRC MSS 126/TG/X/11. Bevin General Correspondence: Bevin to Scoulding, 7 November 1930.

18 MRC MSS 126/TG/1887/3. Bevin to Scoulding, Area 1 Secretary, 23 November 1929.

19 MRC MSS 126/TG/RES/GW/18/4 file covering agreements with Crosse and Blackwell 1926–40; Devenay's report to General Workers Quarterly Meeting, 29 February 1930; *Daily Worker* 6, 7, 8 and 9 January 1930.

day a lightning strike at Union Cold Storage at Lambeth in London against the dismissal of a worker, returning a week later under pressure from the TGWU.[20] the union is also reported as having intervened to halt a strike on Cardiff tramways against speed-up, with management requiring drivers to complete journeys within reduced times. At the same time tramway workers in both Manchester and Glasgow were considering action on the same issue. At Mond's giant ICI plant at Billingham on Tees-side, 3,000 workers are reported as being laid off in a rationalisation scheme approved by the TGWU. There are also reports from London bus garages, Old Kent Road, Hornsea and Croydon about TGWU-approved speed-up by Lord Ashfield's bus combine and a protest from the London Cab branch at the enforced appointment of a branch secretary by Transport House.[21]

Bevin's survival strategy for the union was almost entirely dependent on agreements with major firms. There were virtually no official strikes during this period, the only major exception being the five week transport strike in Dublin. While TGWU representation on JICs did enable it on occasion to reduce or even prevent wage reductions, its overall policies depended not just on preventing strikes but also often on co-operation with firms in the management of work intensification and often quite brutal rationalisations.[22] Those members opposing these policies tended to be marginalised if not expelled. And, in parallel, Bevin sought the political exclusion from the union and from its affiliated trades councils and Labour parties of those arguing socialist positions, whether from the CP, the ILP or their Left allies.[23]

While it would be quite wrong to put the whole blame on Bevin for the depoliticisation of the Labour movement in this period, he certainly contributed. The repeated interventions at branch level had a numbing effect on political discussion and wider solidarity. At a time when the Labour government itself was swinging, ultimately disastrously, to the Right, this represented a major blow for a trade union movement that had, just ten years before, harboured such ambitious hopes for social transformation and possessed a potential for mass community mobilisation that had been amply demonstrated in 1926.

20 *Daily Worker*, 10 January 1930.

21 *Daily Worker*, 8, 20 and 22 January 1930.

22 *The TGWU Record* General Workers pages for October 1930 and March and April 1931 show the TGWU negotiators using JICs in the West of England woollen industrial and for Paint and Varnish to diminish and delay wage cuts.

23 Andrew Flinn, 'Labour's Family: Local Labour Parties, Trades Unions and Trades Councils in cotton Lancashire 1931–1939', in Matthew Worley, *Labour's Grassroots* (Ashgate, 2005) provides some information; Noreen Branson, *History of the Communist Party of Great Britain 1927–1941* (Lawrence and Wishart, 1985) examines the campaign to purge trades councils and disaffiliate left-wing Labour Parties, particularly in London, in the late 1920s.

The 1929 Dublin Tram Dispute:
A Forgotten Strike and Lockout

Alex Klemm

The TGWU leadership backs its Irish membership and demonstrates, in what became the biggest industrial dispute of 1929, the importance of maintaining a powerful central trade union organisation

Bookended by the iconic 1913 Dublin tramway strike and lockout, and the 1935 tramway strike, the 1929 strike – or lockout – has been largely forgotten. Yet it dominated news headlines at the time and focused attention not only on the industrial issues which prompted the dispute, but also on the wider issues surrounding transport infrastructure in Dublin city and county.

On 15 August 1929 approximately 2,000 members of the Amalgamated Transport and General Workers' Union (ATGWU: as the TGWU was titled in Ireland) employed by the Dublin United Tramways Company (which operated both trams and omnibuses) took strike action in protest at a proposed 10 per cent wage cut.

The dispute was to last five weeks. While it ended with the workers accepting a one shilling wage cut, on top of a five shilling cut imposed the year before, the Tribunal of Inquiry which led to resolution of the dispute not only rejected the company's demands, but in its recommendations also laid the foundations for what would eventually become Ireland's public transport system.

The strike took place during a period of relative inter-union amity. The differences between the two main general workers' unions, the Irish Transport and General Workers Union (ITGWU) and ATGWU, dating back to 1922 had largely been papered over by the late 1920s, although they were to flare up again in 1933 and come to a head during the 1935 tramway strike. In 1929, the ITGWU was in a period of decline with national membership estimated at just 15,000 and the ATGWU was the main union in the company (Cody, O'Dowd and Rigney, *the Parliament of Labour: 100 Years of the Dublin Council of Trade Unions*, Dublin 1986)

On the first day of the stoppage, a mass meeting of workers was held in the Trades Hall on Capel Street and passed a resolution expressing full support for the union and the action. According to the ATGWU, between 1,600 and 1,700 members attended the meeting. In a statement issued after the meeting, the union summed up the men's grievances:

> The company persisted, and still persist, in seeking to impose a 10 per cent reduction in the wages of the men [which are] such that they cannot possibly afford another reduction with the consequent depression in their standard of living. Last year they accepted a reduction in wages of 5s per week. In addition to this they have in other ways, by increased speed and alteration in schedules, made a very considerable contribution to meet the difficulties of the company. This is shown by the very large reduction in the working expenses of the company last year. The men are firmly convinced that a further reduction in wages affords no solution to the difficulties with which the company state they are confronted. This contention is borne out by the facts. The Executive Council have decided to officially support the members in resisting the wage reduction. (*Irish Times*, 16 August 1929)

Members of the TGWU Executive Council along with the National Secretary of the union's Passenger Group, Harold Clay, were centrally involved throughout the dispute. The first mass meeting of the men was addressed not only by Clay, but also by T&G assistant general secretary John Cliff, himself a former tramway man, and Executive Council members J. Berry and Herbert Kershaw.

The two Executive Council members initially met with the company and representatives of the Ministry of Industry and Commerce, but noted that that '[i]t was not possible to reach an amicable settlement' and stressed that 'the company must obtain the relief they are seeking from other sources than the wages of its employees' (*Irish Times*, 16 August 1929).

Both during the dispute and at the subsequent court of inquiry, the union sought to place the dispute within the wider context of the problems besetting Dublin's transport infrastructure, and explicitly advocated for public regulation of transport in the city as outlined in their initial statement:

> The union feel that the present position of the transport services requires careful investigation by the Government in an effort to secure, if one may use a fashionable term, a rationalised system of transport. Road passenger transport, the union feels, is a necessary public service and as such it should be subject to a measure of public control. This would ensure orderly development, good public service, an opportunity to the employers, under efficient management, for a reasonable return on capital, and to the employees a reasonable rate of wages and conditions of service.

Notwithstanding the often fractious relations at the time between the ATGWU and other unions, support from the rest of the trade union movement was forthcoming. A meeting of the Dublin Trades Union and Labour Council resolved 'that a committee be formed representative of the different unions catering for the employees of the Dublin United Tramways Company Ltd., outside of the ranks of the Amalgamated Transport Union; that the functions of such committee shall be to assist and advise the strike committee, to act in consort with them, and to take such steps from time to time on behalf of their different unions as may be considered necessary by such committee to secure victory for the workers'.

ATGWU Irish Secretary George Gillespie noted that 'the trade union movement in Dublin is behind this dispute', and told the *Irish Times* that, while there was initially no question of extending the strike, and the men in the power house belonging to other unions would continue working so that services could be resumed immediately in the event of a resolution, 'if the company attempted to run a single tramcar it would be taken for granted that those men in the power house would be called on to cease work in sympathy with the strikers' (*Irish Times*, 24 August 1929).

The leader of the Irish Labour Party, Thomas O'Connell, was understood to have attempted an intervention together with T.J. McKenna, chair of the trades council. Ten days into the strike, a proposal from the Minister for Industry and Commerce for 'arbitration' was rejected. At the same time, there was growing pressure for a 'court of inquiry' into the whole issue of transport. The *Irish Times* reported that a meeting of the men rejected the concept of arbitration, since it would mean agreeing in principle to a reduction of wages, but were prepared to participate in an enquiry into the whole issue of transport in Dublin city and county (*Irish Times*, 26 August 1929)

On August 28, the *Irish Times* reported that the Minister for Industry and Commerce has written to both the company and the union announcing his intention to set up a court of inquiry under the 1919 Courts Act to inquire into the causes and circumstances of the dispute and report to him; he asked the company to agree to 'immediate resumption of the tramway services on the basis of the status quo prior to the stoppage'. The company rejected the Minister's request that services be resumed pending the outcome of the inquiry: thus, the workers were effectively locked out. Workers were updated by the union at a further meeting in the Capel Street Trades Hall, and Executive Council Member Herbert Kershaw told the Irish Times that 'the men seemed more than ever determined to hold out for their rights' (*Irish Times*, 28 August 1929).

The court of inquiry was scheduled to hold its first meeting on Monday 2 September; the workers were due to be represented by Harold Clay, National Secretary of the T&G Passenger Group. Like John Cliff, Clay was himself a former tram driver. A committed socialist, he had been active in the Social Democratic Federation and its successor, the BSP, before the latter affiliated to the Labour Party, a move Clay supported. After his union, the UVW, merged with the T&G in 1922 he became the union's first area secretary in Yorkshire. In 1933 he was to write a pamphlet on 'Workers' Control' of industry, published by the Socialist League.

Speaking to the *Irish Times* as the union concluded payment of a second week's strike pay, Clay reiterated the union's position that the inquiry must address 'all matters relative to transport in the City and County of Dublin', but adopted a conciliatory tone noting that he thought the company was entitled to relief on the rates it had to pay on the track as well as buildings, as well as in other respects (*Irish Times*, 30 August 1929) Putting forward the workers' case to the Inquiry, Harold Clay noted that the wages paid to the men before the war and for long afterwards were not only less than those paid to other tram workers, but considerably below the cost of living figure. While he agreed that wages since 1921 had exceeded the cost of living figures, he referred to the 5s pay cut in 1927 and reiterated the union's position that 'the company would have to look somewhere else for relief than the method they had adopted'.

Pointing out that the men were prepared to continue working on their old terms, Clay told the inquiry that what was involved was not a dispute, but a lockout (*Irish Times*, 7 September 1929). Interestingly, in a Dáil debate the following year on the 1929 Local Government (Dublin) Bill, Sean Lemass – no friend of the tramway men, as he showed when Minister for Industry and Commerce during the 1935 tramway dispute – also referred to the dispute as a 'lockout' (*Dáil Debates*, 7 February 1930). At the conclusion of the enquiry, tribunal chair Judge Cahir Davitt suggested that services be restarted on the basis of the previous status quo pending while the court considered its report which was expected to take at least ten days.

However, addressing a meeting of the tramway men, Harold Clay indicated that the company had advised him that it was not prepared to resume services except on the basis of a reduction in wages. The meeting was also addressed by T&G National Officer George Gleave. Members unanimously supported the position advanced by Clay at the conclusion of the inquiry to the effect that they were prepared to resume work on the basis of the status quo ante and leave the court free to reach a decision in other than a strike atmosphere (*Irish Times*, 10 September 1929).

The inquiry report was due to be presented to government on 14 September, and it was initially thought that the report did not recommend a cut in wages. By that time the union had completed payment of a fourth week of strike pay. The *Irish Times* noted that, with additional funds available, the union was able to pay married men 24s, with 2s for each child under 14 years, and single men 22s, these figures representing an increase of 4s and 2s respectively on previous weeks. The union had paid out approximately £12,000 – or £3,000 per week – since the start of the strike (*Irish Times*, 14 September 1929).

Following publication of the inquiry report, on 17 September Harold Clay sent a telegram to the secretary of the Department of Industry and Commerce accepting the Court's findings, including the recommendation of a 1s cut in wages. The report had, however, rejected the company's proposal for an across-the-board 10 per cent cut in wages, and the *Irish Times* noted that the recommendation for a 1s cut referred back to an agreement in January 1928 whereby wages were cut by 5s with a further 1s cut to take place in April 1929 – the latter cut not having been implemented.

As the *Irish Times* reported the following day, Clay noted that 'the report of the court of inquiry and the covering letter had been carefully considered by the members of the Union, special attention being given to paragraph 23 of the report, in which it was urged that a reduction of 1s. per week should be accepted' – although the members were also clear that they felt the facts did not justify a change in the pre-strike wages. The paper also noted that:

> The tramway men, despite the lengthy period of the dispute, now in its fifth week, refuse to allow their spirits to be dampened, and yesterday, as well as joining in community singing in the Trades Hall after a mass meeting, they had a football match in the evening at Clontarf. (*Irish Times*, 17 September 1929)

On 18 September, union representatives met with the company at their offices for two hours, emerging at 5 p.m. when, the *Irish Times* reported 'One of the men's leaders dismissed the strike picket outside the building with a wave of his hand. Word was immediately despatched to the other strike pickets in the city, and they at once ceased their monotonous patrol' (*Irish Times*, 18 September 1929).

Under the subhead 'the Men's Cheering Procession', the paper went on to report that – after their usual meeting in the Trades Hall, nearly 1,500 men marched to the union's offices in Marlborough Street 'cheering all the way', where they were addressed from an upper window by Harold Clay:

> He described the dispute as the longest tramway and 'bus strike on record, and said that in that dispute they not only been contending against the reduction which the company sought to impose, and which they had resisted successfully – (cheers) – but they had also been contending for a sane regulation of the traffic of Dublin, which would give the company's employees a decent standard of living and the Dublin public a reasonable transport service at fair rates of charge.

After thanking the public, the wider trade union movement and labour representatives in the Dáil for their support, Clay said the workers regretted the inconvenience caused by the dispute but: 'That was not our fault, but the fault of other people; for we have said all along that we were prepared to continue working, pending inquiry and investigation, on pre-strike terms'. He went on to note that the report of the court of inquiry vindicated the workers' position.

After addressing the workers in Marlborough Street, Clay returned to London. Strike money was paid out for the last time, with married men getting four shillings extra, single men two shillings and boys one shilling. Bus services resumed on Thursday 19 September, with tram services resuming a day later (*Irish Times*, 19 September 1929).

As transport services resumed, TGWU General Secretary Ernest Bevin congratulated the workers in a telegram sent to the Dublin Branch of the ATGWU:

> On behalf of the Executive Council, I send congratulations to tramwaymen and 'busmen on great achievement. Please convey to national and local officers and committees our great appreciation of splendid services rendered, also to local Labour movement for their support. Our thanks are specially due to the citizens of Dublin for sympathy and support shown to the men in their resistance to wage reduction. (*Irish Times*, 20 September 1929 and TGWU *Record*, September 1929: thanks also to Catherine Morrow of Belfast Libraries for assistance)

The strike – or lockout – was over. But industrial relations remained fraught on the tramways and matters were to come to a head again in 1935, when an 11-week dispute was triggered by the summary dismissal of a driver, with workers demanding not only that the driver be reinstated but also that the wage cuts implemented in 1928 and 1929 be reversed. Unlike the 1929 dispute, the 1935 dispute was complicated by inter-union strife and used as an industrial proxy by a range of political actors.

9

The TGWU, Bevin and the Economic Crisis

Between the early months of 1929 and 1930 unemployment in Britain rose from 1.25m to 1.75m. By the early months of 1931 it had reached 2.6m (21 per cent). Elsewhere in the world the situation was as bad if not worse. In the two biggest industrial economies, the United States and Germany, unemployment had reached 15 per cent in 1930. By 1931 it had exceeded 30 per cent in Germany and 23 per cent in the US.

This economic collapse posed an unprecedented challenge to the free market theorists of capital, especially in light of the Soviet Union's ability to maintain full employment under the momentum of its first five-year plan. In 1931 Bevin himself, referring to the minimalist proposals for monetary expansion contained in the Labour government's Macmillan Report, noted privately that 'the Russian Five Year Plan cuts across the whole thing'.[1]

The TGWU, the Labour Movement and the Labour Government

Immediately, at the outset of the Labour government in 1929, Bevin remained optimistic of change. In his New Year message for 1930 he wrote: 'today we have a Labour government in office and soon, we hope, in power'.[2] He praised its work on the widow's pension and unemployed insurance and its proposal to raise the school leaving age. In his address to the TGWU Executive on 16 February 1930 he went further and provided a review which, in its strategic vision, shows Bevin at his best. It also reveals his emerging assumptions about a new corporate relationship between labour and capital that depended in some way on the mutual exercise of

1 Cited by Bullock, *Life & Times of Ernest Bevin*, I, p.434.
2 *The Record*, January 1930.

strength – a strength on the labour side which involved holding the Labour Party to its class roots.[3]

> The year 1929 will probably be regarded by future historians as one of the greatest epochs in the history of our people. We have come nearer to status and power during this year than any previous time during our existence, and yet we are only just at the beginning of the acceptation of responsibility [...] the great institutions we have built, equal in efficiency and management to any that can be found in the commercial world, are a feature of Labour's ability to manage and control [...]
>
> From 1919 to 1926 the Trade Union Movement had to fight a great defensive battle which in money, energy and resolution was unprecedented in the history of our movement, but from 1926 onwards there has been a remarkable change over the whole phase of things. [...] We on our side, in accordance with our tradition and practice, began to apply reason for the solution of our problems, immediately we found a willingness on behalf of the rest of the community to adopt reason. I think the beginning of the change can be said to have commenced with the discussion on the Mond–Turner Conferences, because in spite of the fact that the actual recommendations of those conferences have not been adopted in a formal way, they are nevertheless tending to revolutionise the concept of the relationship in industry.

Bevin then went on qualify this relationship as one that depended on the continued exertion of organised working-class strength.

> Organised capital in its corporate capacity has been compelled to meet organised labour on equal terms [...] the position of Labour in these discussions must be one of continuous pressure and attack, because the other side of the table represents the possessing class [...] the workers have nothing to give except their labour and they must therefore proceed on the basis of securing a greater and greater return from the other side. [...]
>
> The curious thing about this development is that it is not coming in the way people expected. As a result there is an inclination to attack what we are doing, not because the purpose of the objective is wrong but by reason of the fact that it has not just come in the form and way certain people have said it ought to come.

---

3 MRC MSS 126/TG/1186/A/8. Minutes GEC Appendix 1, 18 February 1930: Minute No. 116.

Bevin welcomed the Labour government as a 'wonderful achievement in itself' but then warned that it was necessary 'to maintain a very virile political organisation and especially so in view of the tendency of the capitalist Press [...] endeavouring to turn our people towards other classes even within our own Party. To counter this then there must be a vigorous encouragement and defence of our Trade Union position within the Party itself'.

By summer 1930 Bevin, and his Executive, were becoming far more critical. In July 1930 Bevin condemned the failure of J.H. Thomas, as Lord Privy Seal in MacDonald's cabinet, to draft an appropriate bill on passenger transport, and in August he urged his Executive to pass a resolution calling on the Labour government to table legislation for the repeal of the Trades Disputes Act – promised by Labour in the King's Speech for 1929 but not delivered.

Bevin did so in an environment of accelerating economic crisis within which the Labour government appeared helpless and drifting and the trade union movement thereby exposed. Speaking to his Executive on 19 August 1930 he gave the following assessment:

> It is really beginning to make we wonder as to where we are drifting. I think it would be good if the Council passed a resolution calling on the Government to resolutely deal with the problem of unemployment and expressing dissatisfaction with the present lack of grip.
>
> One thing stands out quite clear and that is that the workpeople must more than ever rely upon the trade union weapon. The bankers and the industrialists generally are already manoeuvring for an attack on money wages. The argument being advanced is, having regard to the cost of living, money wages, particularly in what are described as sheltered trades, are out of equilibrium. This Union must be specially on guard. Every available penny must be put to reserve in order that we may be ready when the crisis comes. I am certain that it will not be very long before there is a general attack on wages. Up to now we have managed, in the main, to resist all the demands made upon our members, but it is going to be very awkward with a Labour Government in office urging arbitration and similar methods and knowing, before we go to the courts, that there is a general attitude in favour of reductions awaiting us.[4]

Six months later the situation was even worse. Bevin delivered his report to the February 1931 Quarterly just a week after the appointment of

---

4 MRC MSS 126/TG/1186/A/8. Quarterly Report to the Executive, 23 August 1930.

the May Committee – tasked by the Labour government, after prompting by the Liberals and Conservatives, to recommend ways of reducing the budget deficit. Everyone knew this would mean attacks on benefits and public sector wages. Bevin noted that over the previous six months the union had actually increased its membership and banked a surplus. But he warned:

> I feel it is going to be almost impossible to steer clear of a wage crisis. At any moment we may get a demand on the sheltered trades – docks, trams, road transport – for what will probably turn out to be heavy cuts in wages, and we must be in a position to put up the best possible fight. Suffice to say, that if either of the sections to which I have referred become involved, last year's savings would go in less than a week.[5]

By then Bevin was, at least privately, highly critical of the government. It had eventually put forward a bill to repeal the Trades Disputes Act but capitulated at the first challenge by the opposition. No attempt was made to mobilise opinion in the country. Its Education Bill suffered the same fate. This would have raised the school leaving age, cutting unemployment and limiting the use of child labour to replace adults. The education minister, Trevelyan, resigned in protest. The transport minister, Herbert Morrison, had tabled a London Passenger Transport Bill which would have taken into state ownership London's largely monopolised buses and trams, but Morrison refused Bevin's call for the trade union movement to have representation on the board. This Bill also failed to reach the statute book. The only substantial piece of legislation enacted was the Road Traffic Act which established a single licensing authority, required the inspection of all vehicles, limited hours and provided for 'fair wage' appeals for those working in the industry. Even on dock decasualisation there was only limited progress. The Maclean Committee brought together unions (principally the TGWU) and the dock employers to consider a comprehensive system of registration, but at this stage no universal system emerged.

By spring 1931 unemployment had reached 2.6 million, 21 per cent of the workforce. It was clear that MacDonald and Snowden had no policies to overcome the mounting economic crisis apart from following the advice provided by the Bank of England and the Treasury. This was that wages and government spending must be cut.

---

5 MRC MSS 126/TG/1186/A/9. Quarterly Report to the Executive, 19 February 1931.

Bevin and the TUC's Alternative

Bevin, along with Citrine, had established the TUC's Economic Committee, in part as a response to the Mond–Turner talks, in 1928. When the Labour government took office, the Committee contributed to the Macmillan report and then in the summer of 1930 further developed policy ahead of the Imperial Conference in the autumn. The perspectives were again largely Bevin's.

The TUC's evidence to the Macmillan Committee had focused on domestic monetary policy. This was to increase public expenditure, not reduce it, in order to generate economic demand and at the same time to devalue sterling to boost exports, particularly coal and steel.

The new submission for the Imperial Conference focused on external trading relationships. In the summer of 1930 the French government had raised the prospect of a federal union for Europe – rather similar in character to Bevin's own ideas back in 1927. Bevin and the TUC now drew back from this idea. Economic nationalism in Europe was considered too strong. Their alternative was for a Commonwealth trading and production bloc. When first presented at the end of May 1930, it was seized on by Lords Beaverbrook and Rothermere, respectively owners of the *Express* and *Mail* newspapers, as giving support to their Empire First campaign for empire tariff protection. The report was quickly revised and, in its final version adopted in June 1930, sought to distance the TUC from the 'empire crusade' and stress that an empire tariff was only an incidental. The main thrust was on state-led economic development. It was focused on how to develop empire resources in a planned and collective way that would benefit the dominions and colonies themselves and feed Britain's industries with the raw materials they needed. Bevin introduced the TUC debate in September 1930 as follows:

> Are we not entitled through the colonial Governments for which we are responsible to say that we will not leave the economic exploitation of raw materials to the tender mercies of company promoters [...] Are we not entitled to stipulate that the development of these raw materials shall be in an ordered manner?
>
> Then when we go to a World Economic Conference and we find that one country has oil, another nation has cotton and another rubber, it is not a case of armies and navies settling the business; but we shall say to the others, here are these resources at our disposal, resources which will be open to you [...] but in return there must be no restriction of supplies imposed upon us [...] We urge upon the government that in addition to the political organisation of the Empire, there should be an economic organisation.

Bevin concluded with a grand vision. 'Let us accept our responsibilities and prevent the exploitation of illiterate races, utilising the great resources under our command not merely for our own benefit but for the advancement of humanity as a whole'.[6]

He encountered stiff opposition. The Left, communists particularly, saw it as a reaffirmation of the TUC's capitulation to imperialism. Free traders argued that the bulk of Britain's exports did not go to the empire – only 2 per cent of coal and not much more of heavy engineering. Bevin's response, in a debate won by the block votes of the big unions, was to attack the dominance of British policy by the interests of the City of London and the international money markets. These policies demanded, Bevin argued, 'balanced', non-deficit budgets to sustain sterling as an international currency. The cuts would be borne by the working class. There had to be an alternative and this meant, said Bevin, state intervention. Protective empire tariffs would be on condition that industries rationalised and cut capacity and costs. 'I believe in organising ourselves'.[7]

Bevin Defends His Record

At the 1931 Blackpool biennial conference, just a month before the fall of the Labour government, there were a range of opposition motions. All were easily defeated. However, Bevin used one for a personal intervention. It was the 'treasonous' motion from Port of London administrative staff which accused Bevin of concentrating power in his own hands. Foolishly the mover strayed beyond the key issue of bureaucratic control and accused Bevin of being so involved in government committees and international missions that he was not able to devote the time needed to union business.

Bevin took the opportunity to outline his philosophy in building the union:

> I helped to build this union in Groups and I have religiously refused to attend Group meetings unless it is a crisis. I think I am right [...] I will tell you why. I recognised the danger, in the first inception of this union becoming a one man show. I don't suppose it is egoistical of me to say I have a forceful personality. I should be no good to you if I hadn't but I recognise the dangers [...] When national secretaries have a problem, I have said [...] Try to get through yourself in order to develop responsibility.

6 Bullock, *Life & Times of Ernest Bevin*, I, pp.442–445.
7 Ibid., p.446.

Bevin noted that he always kept himself in reserve in wage negotiations. Nonetheless he argued that discipline within the union was essential and had to be enforced. He also stressed the importance of the union contributing to the wider formation of policy through the Macmillan Committee, the Colonial Development Committee and elsewhere.[8]

In terms of extra-union activities he highlighted two: working for the election of a Labour government and transforming the *Daily Herald* into a mass circulation daily. He had, he said, spoken at 94 meetings during the general election and travelled 2,600 miles. In campaigning to win a million readers for the relaunched *Daily Herald* he had used his Sundays for the best part of the year, 34 in all, speaking at meetings across the country.

In detailing his work for the Labour Party he underlined the importance he attached to parliamentary representation. He had spoken at more meetings than anyone. It was 'his' party as much as any of the parliamentary leaders. The relaunched *Daily Herald* had equally been brought much more closely under his control. In 1929–30 Bevin had negotiated a deal with a commercial newspaper publisher, Odhams Press, to print a bigger and more professionally produced paper with both London and northern editions. Launched in summer 1930 it was, in terms of ownership, directly under the personal control of Bevin and that of Walter Citrine at the TUC. By the end of the year the target of a million readers had been achieved and in August 1931 the existence of a mass circulation daily paper, now directly under TUC control, was critically important in rallying the Labour Party against MacDonald.

This was Bevin's justification. However, it did not deal with the basic objection of the Left. There was indeed a concentration of power at the centre. It was inherent in the way the union sustained its membership and organised its collective bargaining: industry-wide agreements with employers that generally gave at least tacit assurance that the union would not countenance unofficial disruption. These agreements also, and the trade boards that often accompanied them, tended, as Mary Carlin noted, to reinforce existing differentials and inequalities. And policing these agreements did tend to make for a passive membership. This would have been so even if Bevin had not seen, as he did from 1926 onwards, the eradication of left-wing, minority movement and communist influence as an organisational priority both within the union itself and in terms of the union's influence within local trades and Labour councils and constituency Labour parties.

Equally Bevin's political perspectives, as they matured in this period, were increasingly framed within the institutions of an existing economic system that was exploitative and, in terms of British imperial rule, grossly oppressive. Bevin did understand society in terms of opposing classes and

8 MRC MSS 126/TG/1887/3. Biennial conference report.

saw the supreme importance of protecting trade union organisation. He also defended the term socialism. Yet after 1927–28 the active use of mass, collective action was abandoned. Bevin's socialism would be achieved through parliamentary representation and trade union bargaining rather than any form of rank-and-file class mobilisation of the kind seen earlier in the decade. And in terms of projecting immediate strategic aims within the existing constitutional framework, there was every danger, as was seen with TUC's 'Economic Policy Report' in 1930, that these aims could converge with the slogans of those who wanted to defend a very exploitative order.

Nonetheless, one key strength remained. Bevin stood by his belief in the need to use collective trade union strength to defend working people. Within a month of the biennial conference Bevin's intervention would be of critical importance for the future of British politics and, in this, his union's identity with the Labour Party, his control of the *Daily Herald* and his ability to articulate a clear alternative policy would be of determining importance.

10

Labour Rescued

Ramsay MacDonald tendered his resignation as prime minster on 24 August 1931 and in doing so brought down the second Labour government. The following day he returned as prime minister of a national government composed of Conservatives and Liberals and a small number of Labour defectors. The issue that brought down the government was whether workers should, through cuts in wages and benefits, pay the costs of a crisis in the banking sector. It was largely Bevin who provided the arguments which ensured that the TGWU and the TUC stood firm in their opposition.

Challenging Right-wing Economics

The issue of wages had been a central one since the end of war. Britain's bankers had argued that Britain's economic prosperity depended on restoring the City of London's role as prime international banking centre and called for the return to the gold standard with the pound at its pre-war parity with the dollar. This, they argued, would restore London's ability to attract cash from the rest of the world and in turn enable Britain to lend internationally and boost demand for British industrial products. But valuing the pound at its 1914 level also meant that wages had to come down. The coal lockout in 1926 had been intended to complete and generalise this process. It had failed to do so and throughout the 1920s the over-valuation of the pound meant that Britain's economy increasingly fell behind its major competitors and unemployment remained very high. The resulting hardships produced the election of the second Labour government – which as we saw, Bevin believed would, through state intervention and a measure of public ownership, be able to take the economy back into growth.

This did not happen. The Wall Street crash followed 12 weeks later and resulted in a gathering tide of bankruptcies across all major industrial economies. Hedged in by a majority of Liberals and Conservatives in the House of Commons, the Labour government did very little in face of the rapidly increasing unemployment.

However, it did establish, in December 1929, a Committee on Finance and Industry, chaired by the Scottish lawyer, Lord Macmillan, which was tasked by the Labour Chancellor Snowden to examine how far banking adequately served the needs of industry. Bevin was one of those appointed and it provided him with an important opportunity to develop his skills of argumentation in the field of economics at a time of heightened debate from both the right and the left. The empire loyalist wing of the Conservatives, led by the Rothermere and Harmsworth press, were demanding empire protection. The Lloyd George Liberals had called for government-financed public works to reduce unemployment in a programme partly authored by Maynard Keynes. The Mond–Turner discussions, reflecting the interests of large monopoly corporations, had given support to those who wanted government monies to help soften the consequences of further rationalisation and were mildly critical of the City of London. The TUC, significantly influenced by Bevin, wanted a measure of public ownership and monetary policies, including devaluation, that would ease the flow of finance to industry.

Snowden wanted none of these things. An old style liberal in economics, he believed in balanced budgets and a gold-based currency. Membership of the committee was heavily weighted in favour of financial orthodoxy. Apart from Bevin there were just two representatives of the Labour movement, Sir Thomas Allen, chair of the Cooperative Wholesale Society (CWS), and the Labour MP Walton Newbold. Keynes was also appointed but the other members were mainly bankers, employer representatives and financial experts who followed the City of London line.

The Committee deliberated for 18 months and finally reported in June 1931 just before the final financial crisis broke. Bevin had intervened actively in the work of the committee. He was instrumental, as we have seen, in the submission from the TUC in the summer of 1930 which called for a devaluation of the pound, government spending programmes to boost economic activity and state-led reorganisation of production which would draw on the strengths of the empire and commonwealth market.

Little or nothing of this survived in the final report. As it was being compiled, Bevin noted down some personal observations. 'the minds of my colleagues appear to have been preoccupied with this [wage reductions] from the beginning'. He prefaced this with his own caustic summary of the report's conclusions.

A better summary might be [...] in order to maintain its position in the world it [Britain's financial system] must bring its greatest pressure to bear on the entrepreneur and the worker; it must necessarily ruthlessly bankrupt the one and impoverish the other.

Its mode of operation is what it calls 'healthy bankruptcy' and adjusting itself from the worker's point of view by such an intensification of unemployment and poverty that it gets its way in the end by these ruthless methods; but it does maintain in practical security the rentier. It is bound to produce physical revolution: you cannot on the one hand educate a population and maintain a system by working so ruthlessly through the stomachs of its people.[1]

Bevin went on to comment that 'tinkering' through individual pieces of legislation 'will not do'. 'An adjustment of the system must be called for'. The rentier and the entrepreneur 'took more' in 1930 than in 1907. He presented the immediate root of the problem as the post-war restoration of the gold standard: the 'financiers and businessmen of this country thought it an opportunity for exploiting the world and charged prices which encouraged economic nationalism'. He also noted that one key effect of the gold standard policy had been to make the rich much richer. The inflated profits made during the war, under conditions of high wartime inflation, had been banked at pre-1914 valuations, while the money lent to the government, in the national debt, gained very significantly in real value.

Bevin eventually signed the main report and also a minority report drafted by Keynes. The main report proposed very little. It argued that while a managed monetary system might be a worthy aim at a world level, little could be done in Britain without agreement internationally. Some minor changes were recommended in the size of the Bank's gold reserves and the holdings of the joint stock banks. In the underlying analysis of what was wrong, wage 'rigidities' figured significantly. Keynes' minority report proposed tariffs as a way of maintaining price levels and employment in Britain. Bevin and Allen added an addendum that expressed scepticism about tariffs and argued that they should only be used after state planning and reorganisation had been applied to basic industries and state control imposed on transport and power.

The government paid very little attention to any of the proposals. By July/August 1931 it was focused on an emerging crisis in the City of London which over the previous years had been lending heavily (and very lucratively) to continental banks. As the banks in Austria and then Germany started to collapse, the City itself was now in danger.

1 MRC MSS.126/EB/F1/40/10.

Bevin Leads Resistance to Wage Reductions

In his 17 August report to the union's Executive, Bevin amply demonstrated his grasp of high finance to expose the nature of the imminent crisis and to prepare the union for resistance to new demands for cuts.

> You will have observed from the Press that during the past three weeks a financial crisis has suddenly loomed up in this country, which is likely to have far-reaching consequences. The crisis has not arisen as a result of anything that the Labour Government has done, or to the social policy of the country or even to the cost of unemployment. It has arisen as a result of the manipulation of finance by the City, borrowing money from abroad on what is termed 'short-term' or 'ready cash' basis and lending it on 'long-term' causing several of the big finance houses in London to wobble almost the point of bankruptcy. [...] As usual the financiers have rushed to the Government but they have put up a very good smokescreen attributing the trouble to the social policy of the country and to the fact that the budget is not balanced.[2]

Two days later, on 19 August, Cabinet members were brought back from their summer break to discuss the report of the May Committee on public expenditure. This committee had been appointed five months before in response to a Liberal Party motion attacking improvident government spending on unemployment benefits and blaming the budget deficit for a lack of confidence in financial markets. The report now demanded an immediate balancing of the budget. 'Action must be taken forthwith if public confidence at home and abroad is to be re-established and a financial crisis of the first magnitude avoided'.[3] Swingeing cuts were proposed. Payment for unemployment insurance for all employees was to be increased and unemployment benefit cut. Wages across the public sector were to be reduced – those for teachers by 20 per cent – and spending on health, the police, universities, the military and roads all cut. The following day the Cabinet heard reports of meetings with the Conservatives who wanted bigger cuts overall but less on the military, and with Lloyd George who agreed with the cuts but did not want any attempt to introduce tariffs on overseas goods to increase government revenue.[4] On 22 August Snowden reported on discussions with the TUC. 'It appeared', he reported, 'that members of the General Council had no real appreciation of the seriousness of the situation; their

2 MRC MSS 126/TG/1186/A/9. General Executive Minutes, August 1931.
3 TNA CAB 23/67/16. Report of the May Committee, 19 August 1931.
4 TNA CAB 23/67/17, 20 August 1931.

statements appeared to be based on a pre-crisis mentality'.[5] They had rejected any cuts.

Ramsay MacDonald then reported that he had had discussions with the deputy governor of the Bank of England who stressed that foreign confidence could only be restored by 'very substantial' cuts. The Bank was asked to initiate discussions with the New York Federal Reserve about providing cover for sterling. The answer came back the following day that this could be provided only if the full package of cuts was implemented and if this had cross-party backing. By then it was clear that a section of the Labour Cabinet would oppose and MacDonald indicated that he would seek an audience with the king to discuss the future of the government. The following day he reported on these discussions and his belief that in view of the gravity of the situation, he had 'no alternative' but to offer the government's resignation and to assist in the formation of a new national government.

The firm stance of the TUC appears to have been critical, winning a majority in the parliamentary Labour Party against the deal, including Arthur Henderson who had initially wavered. The following morning, at a meeting of TUC and Labour Party leaders in Transport House, Bevin is described as being 'full of fight'. 'This is like the General Strike. I am prepared to put everything in'.[6] The editor of the *Daily Herald* was instructed to report, in the weekend edition, the fall of the Labour government in terms which firmly condemned MacDonald, Snowden and Thomas and other cabinet members who had joined forces with the Conservatives and Liberals. On Monday the paper printed a declaration from the Labour Movement signed by the chair of the Labour Party National Executive Committee (NEC), Stanley Hirst, Bevin's deputy at the TGWU, and the officers of the TUC and the Parliament Labour Party.

> The proposals to economise at the expense of the poor are not only unjust but economically unsound. They will increase unemployment and aggravate the basic problems underlying the present crisis by reducing the consuming power of the masses.[7]

The statement ended defiantly calling on the 'masses of people to rally to the Labour Movement' and 'its constructive efforts towards the new social order'.

The new national government pressed ahead with its draconian public sector cuts despite popular protests including, on 15 September, a large-scale mutiny by the sailors of the Atlantic Fleet. Nonetheless, despite the

---

5 TNA CAB 23/67/18, 21 August 1931.
6 Bullock, *Life & Times of Ernest Bevin*, I, p.491.
7 *Daily Herald*, 28 August 1931.

cuts, the run on the pound continued and a week later, on 21 September, the government was forced to abandon the gold standard and devalue the pound. The following week it called a general election in which Conservatives, Liberals and 'National Labour' would fight collectively under the banner of the national government against the Labour Party.

'Intensive and Continuous Educational Work'

The election took place a month later on 27 October. Bevin fought Gateshead, previously with a Labour majority of 16,000 and lost the seat. He maintained the Labour vote but his National Liberal opponent had a clear run with no Conservative standing. Across Britain Labour was reduced to 46 seats with the ILP holding just five. Apart from George Lansbury, all previous cabinet ministers contesting as Labour lost their seats. Lansbury now became leader of the parliamentary party. In terms of votes the defeat was less dramatic: a swing away from Labour of 6.5 per cent and an overall vote down from 8 to 6.3 million. But in terms of parliamentary representation, Labour was virtually back to where it was in 1910.

Bevin summed up the issues now before the Labour Movement in his report to the union's Executive in November. 'the Labour Movement', a term Bevin now increasingly used in place of the Labour Party, 'stood by the unemployed, we stood against cuts in the standard of living and we fought hard to maintain a solid front against the financiers notwith-standing the fact that three of our leaders became renegades'. He stressed the need to defend the political role of the trade union movement and the TUC. 'the Trades Union Congress General Council has been the subject of the most vicious attacks [...] the obvious object being to try to drive the Trade Unions out of political action [...]. As a Union we have been singled out for special treatment'.[8]

He noted also the implications for the trade union movement, and its members, of accepting the ultimatum put by Snowden and MacDonald. 'If I had agreed to cuts [...] not one of the officers of this union could have resisted the application of the same policy to every industry [...]. If I had consented to the breaking of collective agreements in the manner proposed and since carried out by the Government, the union could not have opposed the breaking of similar agreements in industry. We can at least say we have maintained our trade union position'.

More fundamentally Bevin addressed the issue of why Labour had lost the election despite defending the interests of the great majority.

---

8 MRC MSS 126/T&G/1186/A/9. General Executive Committee Minutes, 17 November 1931.

One important thing revealed in this election [...] is the need for more intense educational work on the part of the Labour Party [...]. Every progressive party which is attacking the system and demanding change must convince its supporters of the rightness of its policy and programme. The experience of the past proves that the ignorant masses only support us when there is grave discontent [...]. Therefore, we must consider the taking of steps by literature, by meetings and by the spread of knowledge in every possible way in order to get the principles of socialism more deeply rooted in the hearts of the people [...] the experience I have had in my own constituency conclusively proves that we have not captured either the imagination or the intelligence of the new voters [...] it is unwise to rely upon a violent swing of the pendulum [...] because it will just as surely begin to swing back again as soon as we begin to introduce socialist policies unless we proceed to educate the people [...]. There is nothing for it but grim, determined effort and continuous and intensive educational work.[9]

In a letter to Josiah Wedgewood he was even more explicit. 'In my own constituency [...] we had lost almost completely [...] most of those who used to finance the old Labour electoral associations' who he described as the skilled workers, the better class of railwaymen and craftsmen.[10] In response Bevin now became chair of the Society for Socialist Information and Propaganda established earlier in 1931 by G.D.H. Cole.

The question remains, however, how far such institutional and rather academic education could be effective if isolated from class mobilisation on the ground that directly addressed the enormous problems then facing working people.

9 Ibid.
10 Quoted from Bullock, *Life & Times of Ernest Bevin*, I, p.500.

Concluding Comments

The 1920s had seen a transformation of Britain's Labour movement – a transformation in which Bevin and the TGWU played a central and critical part. The trade union movement had emerged from the war encompassing a near majority of the workforce. While the old somewhat bureaucratic leaderships remained intact, strengthened by their integration into the wartime structures for labour management, they were faced by a membership whose primary organisation was increasingly at workplace level and who, using their new strength in conditions of full employment, had become accustomed to taking independent (and technically illegal) strike action. The depth of this turn towards local community and workplace action was demonstrated in the unofficial strikes of 1919, in 1920 through the Councils of Action and in 1921 in the preparations for solidarity strike action with the miners.

This workplace activism carried forward the pre-war mobilisation of the 1910–13 period and did so on an altogether new scale – as was recognised by post-war governments and their advisers. It also directly affected the Labour Party. Prior to the 1920s the local organisational basis of the Labour Party was in trades and labour councils – composed of local trade union branches. As the trade union movement was transformed in size and became locally more radical, so also did local trades and labour councils. Solidarity and direct action became directing principles – demonstrated when trades and labour councils transformed themselves into Councils of Action in 1920 and in the East End of London when local labour councils defied the government on relief scales for the unemployed.

By 1931 this was no longer the case. Local Labour parties had been administratively split from trades councils and existed as independent organisations with individual memberships. Trades councils themselves had to operate within strict guidelines laid down by the TUC and, in Scotland, by the STUC. The Left, in terms of the ILP and the Communist Party, had been isolated as TUC proscriptions banned contact with Left-aligned organisations such as the National Unemployed Workers

Movement. As demonstrated in 1931, locally organised class cohesion had largely evaporated.

No less important, the character of trade union organisation had changed. In 1920 there had been something of a balance between central administrative control and local branch and member-based activism. By 1930 this balance had largely gone – particularly in unions like the TGWU. Bevin's survival plan for the union depended on employer agreements mainly at national level. This required local officials to police these agreements and troubleshoot any local challenges. It also meant, in the early stages, major battles – as in the docks and London buses – to face down those who opposed.

In the 1920s the Italian Marxist Gramsci attacked the trade union leaders of this type of 'institutional' trade unionism as 'bankers of men', the non-political accumulation of members that matched, and did not challenge, the capitalist organisation of society.[1] This description would be more than a little unfair to Bevin and the TGWU. In circumstances of high and continuing unemployment there were perhaps few alternatives.

Yet it was also matched in Bevin's case by a slow withdrawal from the radical politics of the earlier 1920s. Up until 1926 he robustly defended the use of industrial action to bring pressure to bear on government. Thereafter he abandoned this principle. By 1927–28 he had also allowed himself to be manoeuvred into a position where socialism was not just no longer an immediate aim but where his attempts to establish broader political understandings with employers led him to endorse objectives, such as rationalisation and empire level trading and planning, that had little or nothing to do with socialism or internationalism. Some would say, and did at the union's biennial conferences, they were its direct opposite.

Were there viable alternatives? Could the general strike, for instance, have been won on workers' terms?

Undoubtedly, some TUC leaders had genuine concerns about a prolonged strike exhausting the movement's financial reserves. Other union leaders seem to have been more concerned with the drift to Left control at local level. But was there an outcome – short of a risky, immediate assault on state power – that would have left the movement stronger and uncompromised? Very probably – given what we now know about the government's own fears and internal conflicts. A tactical victory on miners' wages and conditions would at minimum have required the restoration of some measure of state control, and in terms of its economic consequences would quite quickly have forced a reconsideration of the disastrous linking of the pound to gold long before the debacle of 1931. It

---

1 Ordine Nuovo, 30 October 1921 from *Antonio Gramsci, Selections from Political Writings 1921–1926*, translated and edited by Quentin Hoare (Lawrence & Wishart, 1978).

would also have left the Labour movement in an incomparably stronger position to insist on its own priorities in determining future policy.

Could 1931 have been avoided? Given the balance of forces by time, probably not. The power and authority of the TUC had been eroded and the remaining left-wingers in the parliamentary Labour Party lacked the cohesion and authority to advance alternatives to those of Snowden and MacDonald – effectively those of the Treasury and the City of London.

Nor was there, at this point, the wider political basis for some kind of Keynesian compromise based on a mildly inflationary currency to boost consumer demand – a formula that depended on, and which economically benefited, large-scale industrial monopolies with the power to control prices. The implementation of such polices by Roosevelt in the US from 1933 depended on support from that quarter and the relative strength of big industrial corporations within the US power structure. In Sweden the ability of the Social Democrats to introduce mildly inflationary Keynesian welfare policies from the mid-1930s was in large part for the same reason: a function of Sweden's rather unique economic structure with highly concentrated industrial monopolies, politically weak small business and farming sectors and virtually no overseas banking. This was not the case in Britain. The City and international banking remained politically dominant.

Keynes himself seems to have been well aware of this. At the height of the crisis, on 28 August 1931, he sent a postcard to Bevin saying his sympathies were with him and the TUC and recommending his own forthcoming article in the *New Statesman*. Bevin wrote back rather sharply. He had read the article: 'frankly I do not know what is the point you are trying to make... I cannot see what the contribution is excepting we are likely to get worse'.[2] Keynes had provided, as usual, a brilliant commentary. But he had not offered any substantive alternatives. As in the Macmillan report, Bevin was ahead of him.

Bevin's ability to provide a practical alternative programme for the TUC did ultimately make it possible to rally a majority of leading figures in the parliamentary party. Without this intervention the Labour government and Labour Party would have been held responsible for imposing draconian cuts on the poorest and most vulnerable, and for directly attacking the trade union movement – and then blamed for the collapse of the currency. It is very unlikely that a minority Labour government could have survived, or that the Labour Party could have been saved from electoral disaster and destructive internal conflict in the aftermath of such a crisis. That it did survive, however diminished, was largely due down to Bevin and his union, the TGWU.

2 MRC MSS 126/EB/F1/42/13. Keynes to Bevin, 28 August 1931; Bevin to Keynes, 31 August 1931.

Section III

Questions for Discussion and Further Thought

- Did Bevin have any scope for an alternative strategy to that of long-term agreements with major employers and employer associations – and a passive membership where trade union officers had to police wage structures that were often discriminatory?

- Were Keynesian-type policies, based on the type of collaboration between big business and unions seen in the Mond–Turner talks, politically feasible in Britain in the early 1930s? What stood in the way?

- Why was there no significant mass movement for socialist change during the economic crisis of 1930–31?

- What did Bevin mean by 'socialism' when, after the collapse of the second Labour government, he called for a great campaign of socialist education?

Index